GW01374630

The Right to Roam

The Right to Roam:
Travellers and Human Rights
in the Modern Nation-State

By

Dualta Roughneen

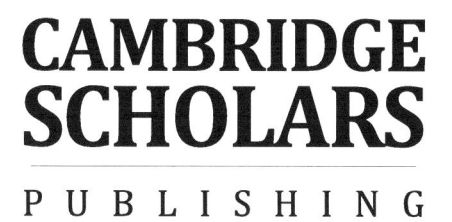

**CAMBRIDGE
SCHOLARS**

PUBLISHING

The Right to Roam:
Travellers and Human Rights in the Modern Nation-State,
by Dualta Roughneen

This book first published 2010

Cambridge Scholars Publishing

12 Back Chapman Street, Newcastle upon Tyne, NE6 2XX, UK

British Library Cataloguing in Publication Data
A catalogue record for this book is available from the British Library

Copyright © 2010 by Dualta Roughneen

All rights for this book reserved. No part of this book may be reproduced, stored in a retrieval system, or transmitted, in any form or by any means, electronic, mechanical, photocopying, recording or otherwise, without the prior permission of the copyright owner.

ISBN (10): 1-4438-1871-2, ISBN (13): 978-1-4438-1871-1

TABLE OF CONTENTS

Acknowledgements vii
List of Abbreviations ix
Summary xi

Introduction 1

Part I: The Legal Evolution

Chapter One 8
The Development of International Law

Chapter Two 10
International Bodies and Treaties to which Ireland is a Member

Chapter Three 15
Relevant Legislation in Ireland

Part II: A Substantive Approach to the Right to Live a Nomadic Life

Chapter Four 24
The Development of the Idea of Human Rights

Chapter Five 26
Substantive Approaches to Human Rights

Chapter Six 28
Personhood & Practicalities

Chapter Seven 30
Normative Agency

Chapter Eight 32
Autonomy

Chapter Nine 37
Liberty

Chapter Ten 41
Minimum Provision

Part III: The Right to be Nomadic

Chapter Eleven 46
Liberty, Autonomy and Minimum Provision of Nomadic Persons

Chapter Twelve 50
Nomadism and Minimum Provision

Chapter Thirteen 52
Nomadism and Liberty

Chapter Fourteen 62
Nomadism and Autonomy

Chapter Fifteen 69
Nomadism, Autonomy, Recognition and Oppression

Part IV: Equality and the Right to Live a Nomadic Life

Chapter Sixteen 82
Universality and Minority Rights

Chapter Seventeen 89
Equality and Nomadism

Chapter Eighteen 97
Substantive Equality and Nomadism in Legislation

Conclusion 103
Notes 107
Bibliography 121
Index 127

ACKNOWLEDGEMENTS

I would like to thanks the following for their assistance and advice in preparing this volume: Mary Rose Walker, Micheal O hAodha, Judith Okely, Jean Pierre Liegeois, John Acton, Camilla Nordberg, Martin Collins and all at Pavee Point, Jim O Brien and the Bray Traveller Community Development Group. Special thanks to Iseult Honohan & Adina Preda.

LIST OF ABBREVIATIONS

CERD	Committee on the Elimination of Racial Discrimination
CO	Concluding Observations
CoE	Council of Europe
ECHR	European Convention for the Protection of Human Rights and Fundamental Freedoms
ECtHR	European Court of Human Rights
FCNM	Framework Convention for the Protection of National Minorities
GR	General Recommendations
HRC	Human Rights Committee
ICCPR	International Covenant on Civil and Political Rights
ICESCR	International Covenant on Economic Social and Cultural Rights
ICJ	International Court of Justice
IHRC	Irish Human Rights Commission
LA	Local Authority
LTACC	Local Traveller Accommodation Consultative Committee
NTACC	National Traveller Accommodation Consultative Committee
TAP	Traveller Accommodation Programme
UDCD	Universal Declaration on Cultural Diversity
UDHR	Universal Declaration of Human Rights
UNESCO	United Nations Educational, Scientific and Cultural Organization

Summary

In Ireland, and in most of the modern world, sedentary living is accepted as the norm, and transient groups across Europe are pathologised as inferior and abject. Recent legislation in Ireland has rendered the possibility of leading a transient lifestyle virtually impossible as the distribution of private and public property is suited to the demands of sedentary living. The right to live a nomadic life is a valid lifestyle choice, and one that is important to Traveller groups. When human rights are viewed as protections of our status as normative agents then denial of the freedom to pursue an important conception of a worthwhile life threatens this status. When nomadism is restricted or denied, not only is liberty infringed but the autonomy of those to whom the lifestyle choice is important is threatened through denial of this conception, and also through a lack of recognition of this important aspect of their identity. Many Irish Travellers continue to attempt to live a transient lifestyle, and those Travellers who have ceased Travelling remain identified through their nomadic tradition. The availability of nomadism as a conception of a worthwhile lifestyle and the liberty to pursue this conception are important in protecting the status of those who value such a lifestyle as normative agents. In Ireland, recognition of Travelling as a valid lifestyle choice requires attaining a balance between the demands of a sedentary majority and a transient minority. As a protection of normative agency, a human right to maintain a travelling lifestyle ensures the requirements of the transient minority are not subsumed beneath legislation and policy that promotes only sedentary living as a valid conception of a worthwhile life. When providing for a right to live a nomadic life, for groups to whom this lifestyle is especially valuable, such as Irish Travellers, a substantive conception of equality would disallow the imposition of legislation which subordinates status groups to the exigencies of majority society. For Travellers, legislation which marginalises Travelling, for the benefit of sedentary society would be viewed as unconstitutional were a substantive view of equality to be interpreted by the courts. The 2002 Housing (Miscellaneous Provisions) Act is one such act, rendering a transient lifestyle virtually impossible, while at the same time, criminalising those it affects most, not just for what they do, Travelling, but for who they are, Travellers. A substantive view of equality, which considers the impact of legislation on autonomy, as a means by which groups are subordinated, should provide for ensuring the autonomy of Travellers is protected through facilitating the possibility of leading a nomadic life, balanced with the requirements of sedentary society, not subsumed beneath the demands of sedentarism.

INTRODUCTION

The conflict between a sedentary lifestyle and nomads can be traced to the 'dawn of mankind'. The battle between Cain, the 'tiller of the ground' and Abel, the 'keeper of sheep', is one of the first articulations of a contest that perpetuates itself to this very day.

> "Now Abel was a keeper of sheep, and Cain a tiller of the ground. In the course of time Cain brought to the LORD an offering of the fruit of the ground, and Abel brought of the firstlings of his flock and of their fat portions. And the LORD had regard for Abel and his offering, but for Cain and his offering he had no regard. So Cain was very angry, and his countenance fell. The LORD said to Cain, 'Why are you angry, and why has your countenance fallen? If you do well, will you not be accepted? And if you do not do well, sin is couching at the door; its desire is for you, but you must master it.' Cain said to Abel his brother, "Let us go out to the field." And when they were in the field, Cain rose up against his brother Abel, and killed him."[1]

The conflict between sedentarised groups and nomadic peoples exists in Africa, the Middle East, across Europe, Australia, Canada, and in Ireland. In Africa, the Tauregs of Algeria and Morocco are an example of a nomadic people struggling to maintain a nomadic lifestyle in the face of the establishment of the nation-state whose borders cut across their traditional pastoral routes. The perpetual conflict in Darfur continues to be defined as one with its roots in the spread of desertification and increasing pressure on nomads to impinge on lands of settled farmers further south. Often ignored in the Middle East conflict, the establishment of the State of Israel has resulted in the marginalization of the Bedouin nomads in the Negev desert. The Aboriginal people of Australia have had their nomadic way of life decimated by the colonization of the sub-continent, resulting in elevated levels of suicide, depression and alcoholism. Inuit hunters in the Arctic in Canada base their existence on nomadic and semi-nomadic herding of reindeer and live in conditions in Northern Canada, with health indicators similar to those in developing countries. The primary example in Europe is the continued marginalization and discrimination of Roma Gypsies in Eastern Europe, and the increasing discrimination experienced in Western Europe as the Roma population escapes from behind the 'Iron

Curtain', facilitated by the accession of Eastern European countries to the European Union and the freedom of movement this brings. In Ireland, the competition between sedantarism and nomadism is manifested in the demands of the Irish Travellers[2] to be allowed to maintain their traditional lifestyle.[3] Throughout the world it is considered that there are three categories of nomadic peoples: 'pastoral nomads, nomadic hunter-gatherers, and peripatetic service nomads'.[4] The Irish Traveller is part of the third group, often referred to as 'commercial nomads'. It is possible to attempt to sub-divide Irish Travellers into a number of broad categories.

> "There are: full-time Travellers who travel more or less throughout the year; seasonal Travellers who travel all or most of the summer but return to a base in winter; holiday Travellers who are basically settled but travel in caravans for a few weeks in the summer; special occasion Travellers who are basically settled but travel in caravans for family or other occasions; and settled Travellers who travel little or at all but still regard themselves as Gypsies or Travellers. Full-time and longer seasonal travelling is most closely geared to work opportunities; most travelling seems to be related to some clear purpose, whether economic, social or cultural."[5]

There are currently 22,369 Travellers in Ireland, making up less than one per cent of the population.[6] Of these, 5,543 are considered to be living in temporary accommodation, either on official or unauthorized transient sites.[7] While the relative numbers of this group seem small, popular discourse continues to centre on the activities and actions of this small group, as well as attitudes of settled society, in the media, in local and national government, and in daily discourse.

In each case, nomadism involves movement. It does not require that the nomad is of no fixed abode; however the nomad lives a transient lifestyle. Pastoral nomads move flocks of animals from place to place seasonally, in response to the needs of the flocks. This usually follows a regular, seasonal pattern. The Turkana in Northern Kenya, currently suffering from the effects of years of drought, fall under this category, as do the Zarghawa tribe in Darfur, one of the many tribes enduring protracted conflict in the west of Sudan. Nomadic hunter-gatherers also move in response to the seasons- following the migratory patterns of animals and the annual regeneration of wild fruits. The Aboriginal inhabitants of Australia would be viewed historically as nomadic hunter-gatherers, while the San, a group of less than 10,000 in Namibia, continue to live a traditional hunter-gatherer lifestyle. Commercial nomads are usually transitory- providing service or seeking business of a 'seasonal' or periodic nature. The commercial nomad often depends on filling a specific demand in an area, then moving on to another area, once the demand declines. Traditionally in Ireland, where the demand was for tinsmiths or goldsmiths, local requirement would be filled quickly and refreshed at a certain period in the future. In the U.S. today, many Irish Travellers are nomadic pavers. They move from area to area repairing roads and driveways, reacting to demand in the market. In Ireland commercial Travellers attend seasonal fairs and informal markets. Travellers' occupation has been described as 'the occasional supply of goods, services and labour where supply and demand are irregular in time and space'.[8] While nomadic hunter-gatherers are very rare, and commercial and pastoral nomadic groups are more prevalent, even among these sub-categories, there is too great a variability of cultures to be able to consider any one 'group' as a typical example of each sub-category.

Though it is not the subject of this volume, it is worth mentioning that the history and origins of the Irish Traveller remain obscure. There are many theories and debates as to the origins of the Irish Traveller. The 1963 Commission on Irish Travellers did not acknowledge the possibility or the theory that Irish Travellers were a separate historical group. The Commission presented the Travellers as a group who had descended from Irish Society, or who had somehow 'dropped out' of mainstream society.

> "The existence of itinerants in Ireland has been ascribed to many causes. It is said that they are the descendants of the remnants of Irish tribes dispossessed in the various plantations. Some are said to be the descendants of the journeying craftsmen and metal workers who travelled the country centuries ago. Others are said to be the descendants of those who were driven to a wandering way of life because of the poverty and distress caused by the famines of the last century, the oppressions of the penal law era and earlier. It is likely that a combination of all these factors to a greater or lesser degree was responsible for the greater number of those now on the road."[9]

The Commission, while placing a negative connotation on the origins of Travellers, portraying the groups as society's failures, the weak who could not keep pace with change, the Commission also attempted to dispel the idea that Travellers are a single, homogeneous group.

> "Itinerants (or travellers as they prefer themselves to be called) do not constitute a single homogenous group, tribe or community within the nation although the settled population are inclined to regard them as such. Neither do they constitute a separate ethnic group. There is no system of

unified, authority or government and no individual or group of individuals has any powers or control over the itinerant members of the community."[10]

Other theories have attempted to associate the Irish Travellers with Travellers in the UK, and with the Roma-Gypsy Traveller groups who have dispersed to most corners of Europe, possibly originating in Northwestern India in the 13th century. This theory has largely been discredited through a variety of channels, one being an examination of the comparative linguistic history of both groups. It is ironic that while the Irish Traveller struggles for recognition as a status group, the dispersed Roma-Gypsy group has become regarded as a transnational minority, with special representation at the European Union and the Council of Europe.

Regarding the Romany in Central and Eastern Europe, Barany points out that

"they comprise an extremely diverse ethnic group that can be differentiated according to lifestyle (peripatetic or sedentary), tribal affiliation, occupation, language, religion, and the date of arrival in a given country."[11]

The geographical scope and the diversity of occurrence of this 'group' creates a challenge in articulating a coherent political approach to a group that is the largest minority across the European Union, yet exist in differing, yet similar, circumstances in so many countries.[12] Barany further points out another complication when considering the Roma populations; 'some ethnic communities, like the Roma, are so deeply split along occupational, tribal, or other lines that one organization could not possibly articulate all their interests'.[13] One commonality running through Gypsy-Traveller and Roma groups is that they continue to be marginalized, historically persecuted and have been subject to severe racism, social and economic disadvantage, and, forced population movement.[14] Linguistically, the Roma/Gypsy Travellers do not share a credible identity- the Irish Traveller and English Traveller speak both English, and different 'group' languages (in Ireland 'cant' or 'gammon' is the common term to describe the language of the Traveller), while the various Romany populations throughout central and eastern Europe, even within countries, speak different versions of the language which are unintelligible to other 'tribes'.[15] There is even a question mark over the reality of a Romany nationalism, and Kovats believes that 'creating' a nationality for such diversity, is dangerous, in that it will further marginalize the group(s).[16] Though the Roma-Gypsy groups continue to struggle against marginalization throughout Europe, they are recognized as a distinct ethnic group despite such diversity, while the Irish Traveller, considered distinct, and generally homogeneous, in everyday discourse, struggles for such recognition.

Irish Travellers continue, even in modern-day Ireland, a country that, until 2008, considered itself to be one of the most modernised and progressive countries in the western world, to seek to find space- physical, societal and legal- that provides for a right to live a nomadic lifestyle, a lifestyle that they have maintained for centuries.

> "You ask any Traveller and they will tell you. We have been doing it for centuries and why can't we do it now. What's so different about Ireland now? What's today's Ireland from the past when it wasn't an issue for Travellers to travel."[17]

Travellers feel that their way of life is being eroded and marginalized by sedentary society, as it no longer fits in with the modern view of Ireland.

> "Travellers were needed to fix their buckets and the like, to do the spuds or whatever. They used to love to see the Traveller coming. They'd even wait. Things are changed. Travellers are not wanted anymore. You have to stop being a Traveller cos the settled person doesn't want you any more."[18]

In order to retain a transient lifestyle Travellers are seeking recognition of this lifestyle through the enacting of policy and legislation that does not marginalize or inhibit Travelling. This requires a network of transient halting sites around the country which provides for both short-term and longer-term residence. Public and private land is managed at present in a manner such that there is limited space available for travelling as required by Travellers. Also required is a revision of planning legislation which allows for Travellers to use their own land for temporary residences, as current planning legislation favours 'brick and mortar' housing. Other areas required to allow for a nomadic lifestyle are improved outdoor market regulations. Travellers' movement is essentially commercial and recent changes in issuing licenses for open markets, as well as increased costs of accessing open markets, have made moving from fair to fair economically unviable.

> "A lot of policy documents that have been made between Traveller organizations and various government departments. Those policy documents have not been implemented, sometimes not in full, or not at all, or in a haphazard manner."[19]

While there is an increasing literature on nomadism and indeed on Irish Travellers and Roma/Gypsy Travellers, there has not been a substantive examination of the right to live a nomadic life. Contemporary society accepts sedentary living as the norm and there has been a historical unease with nomadic living especially since the beginning of empire and nation building; this unease manifesting itself in a variety of forms from integration and assimilation of nomadic groups, to slavery and ethnic cleansing.[20] This volume was prompted by a recent resurgence in hostilities in Ireland to the increasing number of Roma/Gypsies in Ireland as well as the on-going debate in public discourse and the media regarding the 'problem' of the Travelling community. As both groups have histories and cultures associated with nomadism, this volume seeks to look at nomadism and whether there is a *prima facie* right for these groups to maintain a nomadic way of life, and how this right may exist alongside the exigences of sedentary living, rather than be absorbed into, or subsumed beneath, them.

The first section of this volume will look at the situation of nomadism with respect to existing law, both international, and nationally in Ireland. The volume will outline the legal right to nomadism as it exists at present and examine this right in conjunction with recent legislative Acts in Ireland. The second section will examine human rights from a normative perspective, based on the idea that human rights are generated from the protection of the status of the human person as a normative agent, requiring autonomy, liberty and welfare. The third section will determine whether there is a *prima facie* moral right to live a nomadic life from this perspective based on the protection of the status of individuals as normative agents. This section will examine autonomy from an intersubjective perspective dependant upon societal and legal recognition, rather than viewing autonomy as a conception of atomistic individuals. The volume will conclude that there is a moral right to live a nomadic life and this should be balanced with, rather than subsumed beneath, the demands of sedentary society. The final section will examine this right that exists for only a portion of society, and how different conceptions of equality can be interpreted to guarantee that a right to live a nomadic life is protected from legislation which subordinates this conception of a worthwhile life to the exigencies of the 'common good' as viewed by a majority sedentary society.

Part I:

The Legal Evolution

CHAPTER ONE

THE DEVELOPMENT OF INTERNATIONAL LAW

While this section will not attempt to cover all aspects of the development of international law that have impacted on nomadism, some of the major developments will be highlighted. The development of international law over the centuries has been anathema to nomadism. During the colonial period, the concept of *terra nullius* was advocated as justification for claiming rights to unused land or empty spaces.[1] John Locke, in his *Essay Concerning the True Original Extent and End of Civil Government* espoused the view that only cultivated land could constitute true ownership of land.[2] Locke proposed that mixing one's labour with the land granted ownership.[3] Nomads were not considered to have cultivated or mixed their labour with the land they occupied, and as such, the land was considered to be *terra nullius*, free to be colonized and acquired for empire.

Vattel, considering the colonization of the Americas, claimed that Native American tribes (Indians)

"cannot take to themselves more land than they have need of or can inhabit and cultivate."[4]

In his *Principles of International Law,* Lawrence stated that

"Even if we suppose a nomadic tribe to have attained the requisite degree of civilization, its lack of territorial organization would be amply sufficient to exclude it from the pale of international law."[5]

Thus, nomads came to be excluded from claiming tenure over land in international law as it developed in theory and practice. In Western Sahara, the International Court of Justice in 1975, debated how nomadic peoples were related to the territories they occupied. The ICJ was concerned with whether, at the time of colonization by Spain, Western Sahara constituted *terra nullius*. The ICJ determined that land occupied by nomadic tribes was not *terra nullius*. However, the ICJ did not consider that the nomadic peoples could claim sovereignty over the territory, instead attempted to determine which state the nomadic people claimed allegiance to.[6] Nomadic people could, however, claim legal title to land within the state. This was the first recognition of nomadic people having legal tenure to land. The International Labour Organisation, through the development of the rights of indigenous people, established that certain nomadic tribes did have 'collective ownership' of areas of land.[7]

Martinez Cobo defined indigenous peoples as follows:

"Indigenous communities, peoples and nations are those which, having a historical continuity with pre-invasion and pre-colonial societies that developed on their territories, consider themselves distinct from other sectors of the societies now prevailing in those territories, or parts of them. They form at present non-dominant sectors of society and are determined to preserve, develop and transmit to future generations their ancestral territories, and their ethnic identity, as the basis of their continued existence as peoples, in accordance with their own cultural patterns, social institutions and legal systems."[8]

However, this was not recognition of nomadism as a right *per se*, merely that certain peoples prior to the establishment of national legal systems did have an effective, and unilateral, attachment to an area through traditional use of the land. Maintaining this attachment, in Canada and Finland, for example, has not required that the nomadic peoples continue traditional methods of using the land. The Inuit in Canada, and the Saami in Finland, use helicopters and snow-scooters, respectively, to manage their herds of reindeer.

Though international law has not established a right to live a nomadic life, decisions in international law determined that nomadic peoples could establish legal ownership of, but not sovereignty over, the land that they traditionally occupied. The impact of this approach is such that nomadic groups, under the auspices of international law, can lay claim to certain rights within a nation-state, which is oriented toward sedentarism, but cannot exist as an independent entity, outside of sedentary society.

Chapter Two

International Bodies and Treaties to Which Ireland is a Member

Though the development of customary international law has not established a right to live a nomadic life, the citations above show that there has been a gradual shift from ignoring the rights of nomadic people over land they traditionally occupied, to an acceptance that nomadic groups have certain rights and a general rejection of the notion of *terra nullius*. More recent human rights treaties, bodies and conventions have continued to establish rights of members of indigenous, traditionally nomadic, groups.

The International Covenant on Civil and Political Rights (ICCPR), Article 27 states:

"In those States in which ethnic, religious or linguistic minorities exist, persons belonging to such minorities shall not be denied the right, in community with the other members of their group, to enjoy their own *culture*, to profess and practice their own religion, or to use their own language."[1]

In relation to this article, General Comment 23 of the Human Rights Committee states:

"With regard to the exercise of the cultural rights protected under article 27, the Committee observes that culture manifests itself in many forms, including a particular way of life associated with the use of land resources."[2]

Article 27 of the ICCPR protects the rights of members of 'ethnic, linguistic and religious minorities' to 'enjoy their own culture'. General Comment 23 confirms that culture is connected with a way of life associated with how land is used. Nomadism is intimately connected with a particular use of land resources in a manner that is different to that of sedentary living. Nomadism is attached to land in a non-permanent manner, and requires access to land on an intermittent basis. Culture, according to UNESCO,

> "should be regarded as the set of distinctive, spiritual, material, intellectual and emotional features of society, and that it encompasses, in addition to art and literature, lifestyles, ways of living together, value systems, traditions and beliefs."[3]

Traditions held by members of certain groups include nomadism. Nomadism is part of a particular mode of living together, and nomadic groups embrace particular value systems distinct to those of sedentary society. As stated in the previous sections, the traditions held by minority groups are fluid and they are entitled to change and adapt with modernity. It is not required that traditions remain archaic, or rooted in the past, to be considered the traditions of the minority group. The Saami have adapted their means of shepherding to suit available technologies, while Traveller groups no longer follow the romanticized horse and cart model of Gypsy Travelling.

The Equal Status Act of the Oireachtas, 2000 states:

> "Traveller community" means the community of people who are commonly called Travellers and who are identified (both by themselves and others) as people with a shared history, culture and traditions including, historically, **a nomadic way of life** on the island of Ireland."[4]

Nomadism is directly related to the culture of Irish Traveller, a culture is rooted in tradition, tradition that is entitled to change and adapt with the times. For communities with a tradition of nomadism, tied to the culture of the community, international instruments determine that the right to maintain such a lifestyle exists. The Irish Traveller, under the Equal Status Act, should be afforded this right also.

The Irish Governments periodic reports to the Committee on the Elimination of Racial Discrimination (CERD) states that:

> "The government's view is that Travellers do not constitute a distinct group from the population as a whole, in terms of race, colour, descent or national or ethnic origin."[5]

It is the government's view that Travellers are not protected under International Law as an ethnic group. Members of the Travelling community are not protected under Article 27 of the ICCPR, and maintaining Traveller traditions and culture, including a nomadic lifestyle, is not a right afforded to the Irish Traveller, when ethnic status is denied.

The Human Rights Committee, in General Comment 23, on Article 27 of the ICCPR, states that:

> "the existence of an ethnic, religious or linguistic minority in a given State party does not depend upon a decision by the state party but requires to be established by objective criteria."[6]

Whether Travellers are considered an ethnic group cannot be decided by *fiat* of the state party, as it seems has been attempted by the Irish Government. Ethnicity is a concept, and like many others, has evolved and continues to be influenced by debate and real-life interaction and observances.[7] The process of defining ethnicity has moved from one which centred upon race as a particular separating factor, through debating the social constructivist approach to ethnic definition such as influenced by social entrepreneurs who attempt to 'manufacture' ethnic division as in the lead up to the Balkan Wars or in Rwanda under Belgian occupation. More recent discourses on ethnicity focus on identification and self-identification, and these approaches regard ethnicity as fluid concept. The debate between a primordial and a constructivist approach continues, focusing on whether ethnicity is something that actually exists, or has been constructed by society. Many commentators including the House of Lords in the U.K. have established objective criteria for the determination of an ethnic group. The Mandla Criteria established by the House of Lords is broken down into the following areas

Essential Criteria
- A long shared history coupled with a conscious sense of distinctness;
- A cultural tradition of its own including family and social customs often but not necessarily associated with religious observance.

Relevant Criteria:
- A common geographical origin or small number of common ancestors;
- A common language not necessarily peculiar to that group;
- A common literature, including folklore or oral traditions;
- A common religion different from that of neighbouring groups [8]

Following such an approach as that taken in the House of Lords, which establishes criteria for determining the ethnic status of a group, and an examination of this approach with respect to Travellers, would render the denial of ethnic minority status by *fiat* of the Irish Government as invalid.[9] However, such an approach has not been followed, though Ni Shuinéar states that "Irish Travellers meet all the objective scientific criteria of an ethnic group" citing biological self-perpetuation, shared fundamental cultural values, overt unity of cultural form and social separation, own field of communication and interaction, self ascription and outside ascription.[10]

In its examination of Ireland's 3rd Periodic Report the CERD says the State

"should take steps to recognize Travellers as an ethnic minority group."[11]

In its report to the Framework Convention for the Protection of National Minorities (FCNM)[12] of the Council of Europe, the Irish Government states that the Irish Traveller is a "self-defined group", and that

"their culture and way of life, of which nomadism is an important factor, distinguishes Travellers from the sedentary population…Travellers do not constitute a distinct group from the population as a whole in terms of religion, language or race, they are however, an indigenous minority."[13]

This acknowledgement of Travellers as an indigenous minority, falls short of recognising Travellers as an ethnic group, thus creating responsibilities under international law for the Irish State toward Travellers as an ethnic group. It must be noted that this concession toward Travellers was given under the FCNM, a framework, rather than a legally binding Treaty.

The dualist nature of Irish law effects that any International Treaty or Covenant is not immediately incorporated into Irish Law, but requires that separate Acts by the Oireachtas be enacted to create laws.[14] The ECHR Act 2003 incorporated the European Convention for the Protection of Human Rights and Fundamental Freedoms (ECHR) into Irish Law. Section 2(1) requires the Irish courts, when interpreting the Law to take account of obligations under the ECHR,[15] which is continually being interpreted by the European Court of Human Rights (ECtHR). Section 3(1) of the Act requires State organs to undertake its functions in a manner that is compatible with the obligations of the State under the ECHR.[16]

Article 8(1) of the ECHR states that: 'Everyone has the right to respect for his private and family life, his home and his correspondence'[17] In accordance with this Article, the ECtHR, in *Chapman v. United Kingdom*, held that there is a positive obligation on the State to facilitate the Traveller and Gypsy way of life.

> "the vulnerable position of Gypsies as a minority means that some special consideration should be given to their needs and their different lifestyle both in the relevant regulatory planning framework and in reaching decisions in particular cases."[18]

Though the case does not state the extent to which the obligation exists, however, by virtue of the ECHR Act 2003, Ireland is required to take this judgment into account in its courts as well as in the functioning of any state organs.

Nomadism has been identified as an 'important factor' in the 'culture, way of life' of the Irish Traveller but is dependent on the identification of the Travellers as an ethnic group to constitute requiring protection under international law, as the Equal Status Act extends to ethnic, linguistic and religious minorities, not to national minorities, the status under which the Irish State officially recognises Travellers.[19] So, if Travellers were identified as an ethnic group, the Irish State would recognise a right to be nomadic, as nomadism is considered part of the tradition of the Traveller groups. However, the recognition of this importance does not identify the right to live a nomadic as a *prima facie* right in itself, it would only be an associated right, contingent on ethnic identification and an association with the traditions of the ethnic group. The following section will look at existing legislation in Ireland and how these legislative Acts affect the possibility of Travellers, as well as other groups, leading a nomadic lifestyle.

CHAPTER THREE

RELEVANT LEGISLATION IN IRELAND

Though there is neither a prescription for, nor legislation forbidding, the possibility of living a nomadic life, there are a number of recent Acts of the Oireachtas that affect the possibility of following a nomadic lifestyle. This section will look at these Acts in conjunction with Bunreacht na hEireann (Irish Constitution) to determine both their compatibility with the Irish Constitution and their effect on nomadism for the Irish Traveller.

The Preamble to the Irish Constitution states:

> "…seeking to promote the common good, with due observance of Prudence, Justice and Charity, so that the dignity and freedom of the individual may be assured, true social order attained ..."

The constitution does not specify what the Irish view of true social order is expected to be. However, Article 3 of the Constitution provides an insight into what the vision of the constitution is.

Article 3(1) of the Irish Constitution states:

> "It is the firm will of the Irish Nation, in harmony and friendship, to unite all the people who share the territory of the island of Ireland, in all the diversity of their identities and traditions."[1]

Article 3 affirms the desire to incorporate and embrace the diversity of its citizens and their traditions. Given that nomadism is acknowledged as a tradition of the Irish traveller, it would be anathema to the Constitution to eliminate the possibility of the Irish Traveller living a peripatetic existence.

In recent years there are a number of legislative initiatives which have been introduced by Acts of the Oireachtas which impact on the possibility of pursuing a nomadic lifestyle. Binchy & Byrne (2002) provide an in-depth analysis of a number of these and of the constitutionality of such legislation, examined on a number of levels.[2] The Act of primary concern is the Housing (Miscellaneous Provisions) Act 2002, and is particularly relevant when examined in Conjunction with the Equal Status Act 2000, the Roads Act 1993, and the Housing (Traveller Accommodation) Act 1998.[3]

The 1998 Act was viewed as a progressive step in recognising the rights of Travellers, as it empowered Local Authorities to provide housing and halting sites for Irish Travellers. However, the Act did not statutorily oblige Local Authorities to provide housing. The Act obliged each Local Authority to draw up a 5 year Traveller Accommodation Programmes (TAPs) with no sanction for the Local Authorities if the Accommodation Plans are not implemented.[4] The Act also established the National Traveller Accommodation Consultative Committee (NTACC) as well as Local Traveller Accommodation Consultative Committees (LTACC).[5] These are committees, consisting of members of the Travelling and sedentary community to engage in the process of developing the Local Authority Traveller accommodation strategies. However, these Committees are given no power of enforcement or influence when it comes to designing the TAP.[6]

The failure of the Local Authorities to provide Traveller Accommodation resulted in large scale encampments, such as at the Dodder River in Rathfarnham, which created a number of problems, as the sites of the large encampments, did not have the services or the amenities suitable for such large numbers of people.[7] The levels of undisposed waste increased, and the site became an eyesore in the eyes of the surrounding community. In the run up to the 2002 General Election, a new Act was rushed through the Oireachtas. This was the Housing (Miscellaneous Provisions) Act 2002. Section 24 of this Act adds a new section, Part IIA, to the Criminal Justice Act 1994, consisting of 8 sections, 19A-19G. While all sections are relevant, Section 19C is most relevant to this discussion. Section 19C states:

> "(1) A person, without the duly given consent of the owner, shall not—
> (*a*) enter and occupy any land, or
> (*b*) bring onto or place on any land any object, where such entry or occupation or the bringing onto or placing on the land of such object is **likely** to—
> (i) **substantially** damage the land,
> (ii) substantially and prejudicially **affect** any amenity in respect of the land,

(iii) prevent persons **entitled** to use the land or any **amenity** in respect of the land from making reasonable use of the land or amenity,
(iv) otherwise render the land or any **amenity** in respect of the land, or the lawful use of the land or any amenity in respect of the land, **unsanitary** or **unsafe**,
(v) **substantially interfere** with the land, any amenity in respect of the land, the lawful use of the land or any amenity in respect of the land.

(2) A person who contravenes subsection (1) shall be guilty of an offence."

This Section, coupled with the Roads Act 1993, Section 69(1) which states:

"(*a*) Any person who without lawful authority erects, places or retains a temporary dwelling on a national road, motorway, busway or protected road shall be guilty of an offence.
(*b*) Any person who without lawful authority or the consent of a road authority erects, places or retains a temporary dwelling on any other prescribed road or prescribed class, subclass or type of road shall be guilty of an offence"

effectively renders nomadic movement impossible save where there are authorized Local Authority halting sites or private lands where the owners have agreed to allow an encampment. Considering the failure of Local Authorities to provide the level of Traveller Accommodation required, the possibilities of pursuing a nomadic lifestyle have become very limited with the introduction of the 2002 Act

At the same time, when Local Authorities are willing to provide accommodation, there is a clear preference on behalf of the Local Authorities for the provision of 'bricks and mortar' housing rather than halting sites.[8] Of the 3,100 accommodations sought by the Report of the Task Force on the Travelling Community (the task force contained no members of the Travelling community), based on the requirements of transient Travellers, 2,200 were recommended to be halting bays. By 2001, 642 standard houses had been provided and only 129 halting sites.[9] As Crowley states "Travellers now have nowhere to camp legally (except for a handful of transient sites), and moving from one camp to another involves nothing more liberating that moving from one criminal trespass charge to another."[10]

The Housing (Miscellaneous Provisions) Act 2002 renders trespass a criminal rather than a civil offence.[11] It gives increasing powers to the

Gardaí to remove objects brought onto land and to dispose of these if they are not reclaimed within a month.[12] It also gives Gardaí powers of arrest and imprisonment for trespass.[13] Binchy questions the Constitutionality of Section 19C with respect to Article 38(1) of the constitution.[14]

Article 38(1) of the Irish Constitution states:

> "No person shall be tried on any criminal charge save in due course of law."[15]

The wording and interpretation of the Act renders one unsure as to when one is committing a criminal offence. The use, in the 2002 Act, of the words 'likely', 'interfere', 'substantially', 'damage', and 'entitled' as the basis of a criminal charge leave the potential offender uncertain as to when a criminal offence will be committed. A potential trespasser cannot be sure what is to be interpreted as a 'likelihood' of damage, what constitute 'interference' with the land on which (s)he is trespassing, whether this is considered to be 'substantial', what are considered to be the 'amenities' one is interfering with, and, who is 'entitled' to use the land. For example, in line with the law of the land, placing a caravan on any land could interfere with emergency services if they required access to the land in carrying out their duties, which they are entitled to do. Binchy states there are two reasons why crimes that are too vaguely defined are unconstitutional.

> "The first is that fail to give a citizen adequate notice of what kind of conduct will render them liable to prosecution…The second reason is that vaguely defined crimes can lead to arbitrary and discriminatory enforcement."[16]

Also, the Act places the burden of proof of consent to use the land on the accused, which is unusual, though not unprecedented, in law.[17] The Act focuses on creating a criminal offence from a likelihood, or a possibility, of an act (damage, interference) being committed. In law, an action in itself has to be associated with likelihood of damage.

> "The overwhelming majority of serious offences requires proof of intent or recklessness and of actual injury or damage…He or she is being exposed to such punishment for *having* done something, namely, acting in a manner that contains (arguably) a socially unacceptable risk of damage or injury."[18]

Merely placing a caravan on land is not likely to cause damage in such a socially unacceptable manner, in a manner that driving a car recklessly is likely to cause injury. However, it could be considered that the legislation be viewed from a discriminatory perspective, that Travellers are likely to cause damage in a socially unacceptable manner by placing a caravan or setting up camp on the land in question.

Binchy also questions the constitutionality of the law with respect to Article 40 of the Constitution. Firstly, he questions whether this law fails to treat Travellers as equals of sedentarised persons. Article 40(1) of the Irish Constitution states:

> "All citizens shall, as human persons, be held equal before the law."[19]

Binchy argues that the Constitution may be violated in two manners:

> "First, that it treats Travellers, as a group, less favourably than others; secondly, that while on its face applicable without prejudice, it is in fact directly targeted at travellers."[20]

The Act impacts disproportionately on the lives of the nomadic Travellers, as it limits and obstructs their chosen way of life, that of a transient, nomadic lifestyle, in a manner that does not affect sedentarised people who do not require intermittent, temporary access to land for establishing a living quarters. Doyle states:

> "the measure, though neutral on its face, effects a discrimination between Travellers and non-Travellers in that Travellers will be penalised for pursuing their way of life, while non-Travellers will not be."[21]

However, the Irish courts, in *Norris v. Attorney General,* did not agree with the argument that a law that impacts one group of society more than another was unconstitutional.[22]

The second manner in which the Act could be found to be unconstitutional is that it is directly aimed at Travellers. Though facially neutral, the Parliamentary Debates regarding the legislation referred directly to the problem of the 'large-scale encampments' such as those at the Dodder in Rathfarnham, by Minister Molloy. In the Irish Parliamentary Debates, 5 February 2002, Minister of State at the Department of Environment & Local Government states:

> "The encroachment on public and private lands by Travellers has been an issue of much genuine concern recently, particularly in those areas where large-scale encampments were involved. Such unauthorised encampments raise issues wider than accommodation matters proper to the Housing Acts, such as issues of public order, intimidation and trespass."[23]

Binchy argues that it is conceivable that the Act is:

> "repugnant to Art.40.1 in treating nomadism as an extravagant personal whim rather than an aspect of human culture and a mark of ethnic diversity."[24]

While it is possible to argue that the legislation is aimed at Travellers who cause damage to property, the reality is that

> "[i]n seeking to provide criminal sanctions…the legislation has in effect criminalised nomadism."[25]

Article 40(5) of the Irish Constitution states:

> "The dwelling of every citizen is inviolable and shall not be forcibly entered save in accordance with law."[26]

This article of the Constitution has been described by Justice Carney in *DPP. V. Dunne* as "one of the most important, clear, unqualified protections given by the Constitution to the citizen."[27] The 2002 Act, by giving increased power of arrest and confiscation (of caravans, the family home of a Traveller) to the Gardaí can be viewed as threatening this constitutional foundation.[28] Section 19F of the 2002 Act reads as follows:

> "(1) Where a person fails to comply with a direction under section 19C (3) (*b*), a member of the Garda Síochána may remove or cause to be removed any object which the member has reason to believe was brought onto or placed on the land in contravention of section 19C (1) and may store or cause to be stored such object so removed...
> (5) The Commissioner may dispose of, or cause to be disposed of, an object removed and stored under this section if—
> (*a*) the owner of the object fails to claim it and remove it from the place where it is stored within one month of the date on which a notice under subsection (3) was served on him or her, or
> (*b*) the name and address of the owner of the object cannot be ascertained by reasonable enquiry.
> (6) Where the Commissioner becomes entitled to dispose of or cause to be disposed of an object under subsection (5) and the object is, in his or her

opinion, capable of being sold, the Commissioner shall be entitled to sell or cause to be sold the object for the best price reasonably obtainable…"

The Act gives significant powers to Gardaí over the dwelling place of persons accused of Trespassing, when the situation involves Travellers and caravans. Casey, J. (2000) states:

"It is clear that the 'dwelling' protected by Article 40.5 includes any premises occupied by any person as his/her residence. It does not seem to be confined to houses or apartments, and – given its purpose – must presumably apply to a mobile home or indeed a hotel room."[29]

From this, it can be considered that a Traveller caravan is protected by the Irish Constitution, and the removal or confiscation of the home by Gardaí threatens this constitutional protection. Though the term 'in accordance with the law' may appear to give validity to such removal, it must be remembered that legislation has to be viewed to in light of its compatibility with the constitution. In *King v. Attorney General* an Act was deemed unconstitutional for the reason that it stoops to 'methods which ignore the fundamental norms of the legal order postulated by the Constitution.'[30]

Contrary to the conclusion of the previous section, that nomadism, as an important aspect of the culture and tradition of the Irish Traveller, should be protected under the various international agreements that Ireland is a party, legislation in Ireland is targeted at Travellers, and limits the possibility of the Irish Traveller leading a peripatetic lifestyle. Irish legislation, directed at Travellers and their nomadic lifestyle has resulted in a nomadic lifestyle involving 'nothing more liberating than moving from one criminal trespass charge to another.'[31] Nomadism is being targeted such that it attacks fundamental constitutional guarantees of equality, privacy, right to a home and due process in law.

Summary

This chapter has shown that International Law has evolved from being anathema to nomadism and any rights associated with it, to recognizing that nomads, in certain instances where nomadism is associated with culture of ethnic groups or traditional ways of life of indigenous minorities, have legal rights to tenure of land. In recent years, nomadism has been recognized as a valid lifestyle but only in accordance with culture and traditions of indigenous minority groups. Irish Travellers, by virtue of their culture, history and traditions are entitled to live a nomadic lifestyle. Irish legislation seeks to attack the right to nomadism in such, a manner that it threatens the fundamental constitutional guarantees of liberty, privacy and equality. The next chapter will examine whether there is a *prima facie* right to live a nomadic lifestyle, based on human rights being generated from the normative agency of the individual.

Part II:

A Substantive Approach to the Right to Live a Nomadic Life

Chapter Four

The Development of the Idea of Human Rights

The idea of human rights came to the fore after World War II with the Universal Declaration of Human Rights in 1948. Since this declaration there has been a proliferation of declarations, conventions, covenants and frameworks outlining the rights humans have, as well as developing the content of these rights. A very small portion of these have been mentioned in the first chapter and nomadism, as a way of life, is not regarded as a *prima facie* right.

Prior to the UDHR, the term human rights came into use in the 18th century with the French Declaration of the Rights of Man and of the Citizen in 1789. However, these rights did not include rights for every human being, and were primarily focused on the male, and the male citizen in particular- a title that was not open to everyone in the country. Prior to the French Declaration, the focus was on 'natural rights' derived from 'natural laws', rights that were innate to the human being by virtue of these being handed down by God and was particularly influenced by Thomas Aquinas. The idea of natural rights developed as man came to consider himself as a co-creator, made in the image and likeness of God, and that our natural rights are those proscribed to protect our role and ability as creators and as responsible agents of God's will.

However, it was Kant who derived human rights (the 'right belonging to every man by virtue of his humanity') from the Universal Principle of Right which states that "any action is right if it can co-exist with everyone's freedom in accordance with a universal law."[1] Kant believed that humans have dignity, a value beyond price, and this dignity required that humans be treated as ends in themselves, rather than means. Human rights, or Kant's natural rights, are those required to protect the dignity of the human, and that (s)he be treated not as means, but as an end in oneself.[2]

It is this idea of the 'inherent dignity of all members of the human family' that is enshrined in the preamble of the UDHR. The much lauded, and quoted introduction, has been used by many groups in the claim for protection under human rights by States in the defence of human rights.

> "recognition of the inherent dignity and of the equal and inalienable rights of all members of the human family is the foundation of freedom, justice and peace in the world... the General Assembly [of the United Nations] proclaims this Universal Declaration of Human Rights as a common standard of achievement for all peoples and all nations."

When considering human rights, the idea of dignity seems central to what human rights are about. However, the 'dignity of the human person' is something that needs to be defined, if we are to understand what human rights are. Many attempts have been made to define this phrase in identifying, and determining the content of, human rights. This volume will also follow this trend in examining the relevance of a right to live a nomadic life, and determining its content. This is not to say that this is the only, or best, approach to determining human rights. Other approaches that can be considered are choice theories of rights, interest theories or more structural approaches. Dworkin proposes that rights are trumps.[3] Rights exist in order to ensure and protect individuals from being sacrificed for the common good, or for a social aim. Nozick also considers rights from a structural perspective. They are viewed as side constraints which "place limits on the permissible pursuits of personal or common good."[4] A structural approach can provide insight into the role that human rights can and should play, but fail to provide an analysis of what human rights are and how we may derive the exact content of human rights. For this volume, in order to examine the validity, determine the content, of the right to be nomadic a recent substantive approach to human rights will be used.

CHAPTER FIVE

SUBSTANTIVE APPROACHES TO HUMAN RIGHTS

Griffin, in *On Human Rights,* is one of the most recent theorists who seek to outline a 'substantive' approach to determining the content of human rights.[1] Griffin also realising the requirement that a substantive approach to human rights requires examining the term 'human dignity' states that:

> "a substantive account of *human* rights, therefore, must contain some adumbration of that exceedingly vague term 'human dignity', again, not in all of its varied form, but in its role as a ground for human rights."[2]

Ingram's 'A Political Theory of Rights' is another attempt at a substantive approach to determining the content of human rights. She claims

> "the job of the kind of theory I am after is to provide a general organizing idea or principle that makes sense of talk of rights and explains how and why certain attributions of rights can be declared valid and others cannot."[3]

Ingram's theory is one she declares to be applicable to liberal democracies and, that

> "this political understanding of rights is that it starts from the claim that autonomy is the value to be secured by rights. That is to claim that autonomy is the fundamental presupposition of our political tradition. There is no claim that it is a universal human essence."[4]

Both authors outline a substantive approach to solving what Griffin declares to be the job of philosophers and jurisprudents; to solve the indeterminateness of sense of the term human rights,[5] as the term 'human rights', he believes 'is nearly criterionless'.[6] These theories, in some ways, assume that human rights, can, and do exist, and that they are more than simply a formulation of highly-esteemed values, that have evolved in the

'Western world', in response to democratisation of empires and their colonies, as well as laying down principles in response to various atrocities in the recent past. Substantive theories need not be a best fit with the legally established human rights, and indeed many tend to question some of the rights that are grounded in that most esteemed of documents, the Universal Declaration of Human Rights.

This volume will examine the right to be nomadic, following closely, the substantive account proposed by Griffin, where human rights are grounded in *personhood*, or, more specifically, *normative agency.*

Chapter Six

Personhood & Practicalities

The idea of human rights being grounded in the *dignity of the human person* is one that has been around for a while. The dignity of the human person means that one should not be used as a means to someone else's, or society's, ends. If human rights are to protect this dignity, we need to define more sharply what dignity entails. Griffin determines *personhood* as the facet that gives the human dignity.[1] What personhood means is grounded in a special facet that persons, as opposed to objects, possess. There must be some particular characteristic that sets humans apart from the other species. Personhood is something that only members of the human species can posses. Theorists have viewed human rights as protecting personhood when it exists. Some argue that personhood is an evolutionary process. This may be true, in that humans gain personhood as they grow and develop, however if human rights are derived only to protect personhood once it exists, essentially a substantial portion of the human species is excluded from this most valuable protection. Thus, in order to have a more inclusive human rights mechanism, human rights ought to protect both the existence of personhood, and its attainment, for those members of the human species that have not yet reached *full* personhood. Theorists, have wrestled with the conundrum of personhood and children- and reached a solution that children need not fall under the realm of human rights and personhood, but rather another set of protections. Wellman believes children's rights, and the rights of others at the periphery of life need not be ascribed human rights as they would be protected through other forms of rights, and duties upon parents or society, in a full rights theory.[2] I find this is inadequate, given the importance that human rights are ascribed

> "having certain social affects, such as ease of transmission and potency in political action…it can facilitate deep moral shifts…lends itself to political slogans… it can empower individuals."[3]

To claim that other forms of rights are suitable for the protection of children or others at the periphery of life, and only affording the particular protections of human rights to the 'paradigm' rights holders, seems anathema to the idea of human rights which have evolved from a desire to protect the most vulnerable in society.

The human species has a particular facet that is considered extremely valuable. Humans can conceive plans for fulfilment, or as Griffin states:

> "We human beings have a conception of ourselves and of our past and our future. We reflect and assess. We form pictures of what our good life would be…And we try to realize these pictures. This is what we mean by a distinctively human existence."[4]

Human rights are to protect our distinctly human existence. Human rights are also to protect the attainment of this distinctly human experience. This criteria still remains vague and requires further sharpening. What this distinctly human existence is, as opposed to the existence of animals or objects needs to be clarified, in order to determine what the rights, and what protections, are needed for maintaining, and attaining, this existence.

Also, human rights are generally considered to be universal- that they apply to all. Every human has these rights. It is claimed that human rights are doubly universal: that is they are rights for all, to be respected by all. If this is the case, and it seems that this should be the case, then the content for human rights must be determined in a practical manner that allows for this double universality. There can only be rights that can exist for all, if they can be respected by all in an equal manner. Thus, the content of human rights for one individual can only be co-existent with the rights of all others so long as it does not infringe the equal rights of another. This balance that has to be achieved can be considered to be the *practicalities* of a substantive account of human rights.[5]

CHAPTER SEVEN

NORMATIVE AGENCY

As the development of a substantive account of human rights has interpreted dignity as lying in the personhood of each human being, it still remains to define what it is about personhood that requires protection by *human* rights. Personhood is loosely defined in the previous section as being centred on the ability of the human person to assess, plan and reflect and realize these plans. Humans are agents. But they are more than just agents who act. They act in a particular manner, a manner unique to the human species. Griffin defines this capacity as *normative agency-* being "our capacity to choose and pursue our conception of a worthwhile life".[1] As normative agents, we have the capacity to conceive, critically, though not always creating a life plan, of what we believe to be a worthwhile life and the capacity to follow through and attempt to realize this idea of a worthwhile life. This is what grounds Griffin's substantive approach to human rights. Human rights are protections of our uniquely human capacity as *normative agents*. Human rights are not rights to a guaranteed flourishing life, or guarantees of achieving the conception of a worthwhile life. Human rights are protections of the austere demand of normative agents to be able to conceive of what one considers a worthwhile life, and pursue this conception without hindrance- retaining the practical restriction that these must be compatible with similar protections for all.

So, what does a human require in order to be a normative agent? Assuming Griffin's conception, conceiving and pursuing a worthwhile life, one firstly, requires the ability to conceive of an idea of a worthwhile life- this ability being something approaching a familiar concept in human rights parlance, autonomy.[2] One also requires not having restrictions placed on individuals when they attempt to pursue this conception of a worthwhile life- liberty.[3] However, while conceiving and pursuing are realised through autonomy and liberty, also required are the basic amenities of life to ensure one is physically capable of pursing the conception of a worthwhile life. Griffin considers this third facet to be minimum provision, or welfare.[4] Griffin argues that if one is continually struggling and scraping for survival it is difficult to be considered a normative agent as time is consumed on survival rather than conceiving and pursuing a worthwhile life.

If we are to consider whether the right to live a nomadic life is a human right, we need to consider whether nomadism is a protection of the normative agency of individuals, and denial of this right hinders normative agency. In order to do this, it is necessary, firstly, to determine and explore in greater depth what is meant by the three basic requirements of normative agency- liberty, autonomy and minimum provision. Though they are familiar concepts, it is necessary that they be better defined in the context of normative agency, in order to develop a theory of human rights. If the denial of the right to live a nomadic life threatens these three facets, and they are no longer protected, then it is possible to claim that there is a right to live a nomadic life on this basis.

CHAPTER EIGHT

AUTONOMY

Autonomy, as a requirement of normative agency, is the ability to conceive of a worthwhile life. Considering autonomy from this perspective, there are at least three components to this- the first is having alternative versions of what may be considered a worthwhile life available, the second is having knowledge of this array of options which can be considered, and the third is having the mental capacities to understand and choose these options. Take away one of these components- lack of availability of options, lack of knowledge of these options, or the mental capacities to understand and choose these, then autonomy is limited, or non-existent.

For example, consider a woman living in a male-dominated society. The woman is aware of many options regarding the life she could choose to live if she were in a different society, but these are not available to her. She is not autonomous as she cannot avail of any of these potential choices. On the contrary, consider a person living in a closed society such as the DPRK, cut off from the rest of the world, grows up with only knowledge of her one way of life, a centrally controlled, socialistic model, which is very rigid and regimented. Her autonomy is restricted as she does not have knowledge of an array of options of alternative lifestyles. While it need not be necessary to have a vast array of options, a reasonably rich array of options is considered necessary to facilitate autonomy.

One can be an autonomous person in the sense that Dworkin describes autonomy:

> "Autonomy is conceived of as a second-order capacity of persons to reflect critically upon their first order preferences, desires, wishes and so forth and the capacity to accept or attempt to change these in light of higher-order preferences and values."[1]

It is necessary to have the mental capacity, when the options and knowledge of these options are available, to reflect upon ones first-order preferences, and revise these preferences in light of reasoning and understanding of what one's preferences actually are. One's initial preference may be to live a hedonistic lifestyle, but on reflection, one may consider a more ascetic lifestyle, as more worthwhile, considering the long term benefits to health and well-being. Or, it may just be the opposite- the question arises not out of whether asceticism or hedonism is the better option, it is that an individual has the capacity to reflect upon initial impulses and form a second-order preference. An autonomous individual is one who is in charge of himself, rather than constantly driven by urges and desires.

> "In order to have second order volitions, someone has to be able to think of himself as a being with a future and a past, a subject of experiences, a possessor of beliefs and desires."[2]

A cat is not deemed to be autonomous in this respect. A cat eats in response to hunger when food is placed in front of him. A person, who is hungry, may want to eat, yet, reflecting upon a desire to watch one's weight, may decide not to. The person should be able to reason that this is a truly preferred way of life, having an idea of consequences, not necessarily a cost-benefit analysis, but an intuition of consequences and preferences. While a cat is not generally deemed to be autonomous, a child, as a member of the human species, has the capacity to become autonomous. While a new-born baby is no more autonomous than tail-chasing puppy, a child has the capacity to develop Dworkin's idea of autonomy. It is this capacity, whether realised or not, must be protected by human rights.

Raz points out

> "If a person is to be maker or author of his own life then he must have the mental abilities to form intentions of a sufficiently complex kind, and plan their execution. These include minimum rationality, the ability to comprehend the means required to realize his goals, the mental faculties necessary to plan actions, etc."[3]

In order to be autonomous certain mental abilities to make choices are required. When the mental capacity to make these choices is limited the autonomy of the individual is affected. While these capacities are attained in degrees by the human species, they can also be limited and removed. Torture is a means by which mental capacities are eroded and is considered abhorrent throughout civilization. Similarly, extreme indoctrination is considered to affect the mental capacities of an individual to act autonomously. Addictions affect autonomy in such a manner that an addict may be unable to revise first order preferences. An addict may be driven by autonomy-restricting need to commit crimes, to forego all second-order preferences, in the order to satisfy the physical first order preferences for addictive substances. There are other factors that limit or restrict autonomy. Lindley gives an example of how mental disorders affect autonomy:

> "There is evidence that schizophrenia is precipitated, amongst vulnerable people, by impossible and contradictory demands being put upon them within the family. Both schizophrenia and depression are destroyers of people's autonomy."[4]

If we are to consider human rights as protections of autonomy, situations which infringe the individual autonomy of the person are a complex matter of concern, especially where it is possible that the effect of these situations are subject to individual tastes, reactions or vulnerabilities. What infringes the autonomy of one person may not necessarily have the same effect on another. Individuals are vulnerable in differing ways and to differing levels to external factors which may impact on their autonomy.

However, our relationships with individuals and society can also impact upon autonomy. Individuals are affected by their surroundings, their interaction as individuals with other individuals and society. Autonomy is linked to recognition- recognition of individual worth by one's immediate society, and self-recognition, which can be a reflection of societal recognition. Honneth explores the role recognition plays in identity and autonomy. He considers the different aspects of identity which are linked to recognition, and are affected by recognition. Honneth identifies three aspects of identity which are linked to recognition- self-confidence, self-esteem and self-respect as *intersubjective* elements which are tied to autonomy. Honneth considers these as

> "three distinct species of 'practical relation-to-self'. These are neither purely beliefs nor emotional states, but involve a dynamic process in which individuals come to experience themselves as having a certain status…coming to relate to oneself in these ways necessarily involves recognition from others."[5]

These three practical relations to self are intersubjective, as they depend upon relationships between the individual and society, and the reactions of individuals to these relationships. Individuals tend to react individually and not in a homogeneous manner. Autonomy requires recognition through emotional support, cognitive respect and social esteem, respectively in order to maintain self-confidence, self-esteem and self-respect.[6] Honneth's arguments are summed up by Kaupinnen:

> "Honneth argues that if we lacked *basic self-confidence*, we would be hindered from exercising our autonomy-relevant capacities, since we would not give our desires and needs the weight they deserve in deliberation…"[7]

When self-confidence is lacking, the individual is not in a position to understand and weigh up desires, or preferences, when in deliberation with oneself, but also with society. When this occurs, one is not truly autonomous in the sense Dworkin describes.

> "…If we lacked *self-respect*, understood as a positive attitude toward one's ability to make rational decisions, our autonomy would be again undermined – we would defer to others, debase ourselves…"[8]

Likewise, when self-respect is damaged by a lack of recognition, autonomy is affected as an individual is not acting under rational preferences, but subordinating his/herself to the preferences of others.

> "…Finally, if we lacked *self-esteem*, understood as valuing ourselves under particular role-descriptions and identities, we would be hindered from undertaking particular projects involving those identities."[9]

Similar to the effects of a lack of self-confidence and self-respect, a lack of self-esteem can limit autonomy- no longer does an individual value one's role in society or one's identity, and becomes reluctant, or unable, to carry out activities that are linked to one's conception of a worthwhile life.

These three subjective elements outline an argument that social perception and mutual recognition play a role in forming, determining and limiting the autonomy of the individual. This seems to contradict Rawls assertion that an autonomous person ought to be a 'self-originating source of valid claims' as each individual should form preferences independent of others.[10] However, individuals generally cannot and do not exist separate from society. Even those that chose to live the life of a hermit, make that choice in society. What is required is the ability to function autonomously in a society, acknowledging the influences of culture in so far as they do not indoctrinate or restrict the formation of preferences. Lindley elaborates this idea, with respect to autonomy:

> "Autonomy requires a person to reflect on the influences of her culture, to sort out those of her felt impulses which are really expressions of her unique nature, from those which are *merely* the product of external influences."

Similarly, regarding recognition, it is when the mis-recognition or disrespect occurs in reciprocal relationships, that self-esteem, self-respect, and self-confidence, are eroded; limiting the autonomy of the individual. Existing in society has the possibility of infringing the autonomy of the individual when one lacks recognition. Lack of recognition can manifest itself in many, many ways- when one is denigrated, when one is bullied when one is shunned, when one is marginalised. The lack of recognition can impact upon some individuals differently to others. While some may be resilient to the effects of bullying, may have coping mechanisms, or find recognition in other circles of society, the same bullying may have greater adverse, debilitating effects on the self-respect, self-confidence and self-esteem on other individuals.

Human rights as protections of normative agency need to protect autonomy, one of the three requirements of agency. Human rights are required to ensure the availability of an array of choices, and to facilitate knowledge of these choices. Human rights should protect and facilitate the ability to act autonomously, which is linked to mental capacities, and dialogical formations of recognition based on self-esteem, self-respect and self-confidence.

Chapter Nine

Liberty

While autonomy as a requirement of normative agency is very difficult to define, liberty ought to be a less contentious issue. However, the concept of liberty can, and does, have various interpretations. John Stuart Mill is possibly the most famous theorist of the topic, with his book *On Liberty*. However, for the purposes of this volume, a particular view of liberty is to be considered. Liberty, with respect to normative agency, is the freedom to pursue an idea of a worthwhile life. One should be free to follow a path in life that one conceives of as worthwhile. While human rights are not guarantees of a flourishing life, nor are they guarantees of success in achieving one's conception of a worthwhile life, they ought to protect the freedom to pursue one's idea of a worthwhile life. However, inevitably, there are always obstacles to be overcome in this *pursuit* of the worthwhile life. It is not always clear what constitutes pursuit, and what constitutes success. Nor is it always clear what constitutes an obstacle in pursuing a worthwhile life, or what is an obstacle to achieving success in attaining this worthwhile life. Liberty as a concept is problematic, in that it is not clear what constitutes liberty in the pursuit of one's chosen worthwhile life. What are acceptable obstacles and what obstacles should society strive to remove? One is only free in pursuit insofar as one can reach. What is acceptably close to achieving a goal? If my conception of a worthwhile life is one having enough to eat and drink, having a few friends and starting a family, suppose I have just enough to eat and drink, and have a few friends, but don't get that family I desire, is that close enough? Suppose nature restricts my ability to make friends, but I have access to enough food and drink, is this sufficient liberty? What if my conception of a worthwhile life is one of being a famous movie star? What level of liberty is required? Do human rights require that I am free to get as close to achieving this as my talents allow? What if other 'obligations' get in the way- such as providing for my family? Suppose my idea of a worthwhile life is to travel extensively? There are seas, and air-fares that get in the way. There may be no official barriers but my lack of money restricts my 'liberty'- my pursuit. But is my pursuit restricted? Or is my success restricted? These are just a sample of the questions.

Intuitively, one would lead to the idea that human rights in terms of liberty refer to negative freedom- the freedom not be interfered with in pursuing what one has conceived of as a worthwhile life. I contend that many of the same questions above will arise again once societal considerations are raised. Is the societal construct a restriction if one's conception of a worthwhile life is not facilitated or considered a paradigm of worthwhile living? However, this negative liberty is restricted such that it cannot override the human rights of others, which protect their normative agency- in the form of liberty, autonomy and minimum provision. A further restriction on protection of liberty as a human right is that this liberty is only the liberty associated with pursuing a worthwhile life as a *normative agent*. Griffin states:

> "what the pursuit of the conception of a worthwhile life largely requires, and what a society might sometimes have some obligation to help provide, are the all purpose means to pursue any plausible conception of a worthwhile life: that is, education, basic health, minimum material provision, help to overcome lack of key capacities etc."[1]

Thus, Griffin is claiming that society is bound to provide for a minimum level of capacity- basic health, education, minimum material provision- so that one can strive to pursue an idea of a worthwhile life- a sense that once you have these you are on your way.

Griffin claims that this requirement only stretches so far as to the level needed to live as a normative agent.[2] Though Griffin creates an idea as to what is involved, the level of liberty required still remains indeterminate. And the conception of liberty is beginning to overlap with minimum provision. While human rights protect the liberty to pursue a conception of a worthwhile life, human rights are not guarantees of the realization of that conception. Liberty requires that one can pursue a particular career, but does not guarantee employment in that career, or success in the chosen career. Griffin attempts to solve this by introducing a threshold level of normative agency, though this threshold remains undefined throughout his text.[3] However confusion remains as to what constitutes this threshold level? How much liberty is needed to achieve this threshold and how do we measure it?

From Griffin, it seems that liberty is not just a right to non-interference; it is also a claim right for the provision of the means to be at liberty. One may theoretically be free to live a nomadic life, yet this could be practically precluded by the acquisition of all land for sedentary living. Intuitively, it would seem that there is some obligation on society to provide 'space' for an individual to be at liberty. What is society required to provide to satisfy this liberty? Griffin declares that "constraint and compulsion are familiar enemies to liberty".[4] The distinction between the two remains unclear. Constrain can often be in the form of compulsion, and compulsion can be created by constraint. One-way-streets compel one to drive in a particular direction, and also constrain the freedom to choose which direction to drive. This constraint or compulsion is hardly a restriction on liberty that affects normative agency, yet it remains unclear which restrictions are. Detention without trial is a significant constraint on liberty, one plausibly requiring the protection of human rights- it is physical restriction on the liberty to pursue a worthwhile life. Attempting to add definition Griffin declares that

> "In order to decide what is and what is not an issue of liberty, according to the personhood account, what can and cannot conceivably matter to whether we function as normative agents."[5]

This declaration however fails to get to the crux of the definition, as functioning as a normative agent is a function of liberty, yet the determination according to Griffin, of liberty is a function of normative agency. Normative agency consists of the liberty to pursue a worthwhile life, yet this liberty is dependant on functioning as a normative agent. This circular determination is problematic in determining the content of the human right to liberty under Griffin's theory.

However, the claim right to liberty discussed above might be better described as the provision and maintenance of a political and social structure that allows the freedom to pursue a worthwhile life. Though, the shape of this social structure remains indeterminate so long as the level of liberty demanded by normative agency remains so. Would predetermining this social structure undermine the right to choose the type of society we choose to live in? What exactly is the claim right we are talking about? When there is a claim right, there is a corresponding obligation? Who does the obligation fall upon? What does the obligation consist of? The content of the right, which at present seems indeterminate, determines the content of the correlative duty. I will attempt to touch on this issue with regard to the right to be nomadic when examining this particular right under

Griffin's theory. As a general outline, Griffin provides six constraints to which the correlative duties to the right to liberty would be subject.

- One person cannot claim a broader range of options than is compatible with an equally broad range for others
- Society will accept the claim right if it is pursuant to living as a normative agent
- Liberty may not require broadening options restricted by nature
- Liberty is not a right to a worthwhile life, just its pursuit
- Liberty doesn't require the availability of the particular form of option that a person has settled on- alternatives can be as good, or nearly as good
- Our options are provided and restrained by nature, culture, and economic growth, scientific and technological advance.[6]

This list of constraints can be informative in determining and limiting the claim of rights holders, and determining the content of that right, in a given context. The list does not solve the fundamental question on the nature of liberty but may be constructive in examining the content of a human right that is derived from a liberty claim.

Many of the aspects, indeed the basics, Griffin highlights as being necessary for liberty fall under the third requirement of his theory, the requirement of minimum provision. The concept of liberty, with respect to nomadism, later in this volume, will seek to overcome this apparent impasse. Contrary to the perception at the beginning of this section, it does appear that liberty, in its abstractness, is a more contentious concept than autonomy, once the extent of liberty is required to be quantified. However, I hope to subsequently show that the liberty to be nomadic is sufficiently important to fall under the protection of human rights based on its impact on the autonomy of those who seek to live a peripatetic lifestyle.

Chapter Ten

Minimum Provision

The final requirement of normative agency is that of minimum provision. Human rights should exist to ensure one can stay alive and ensure access to the basics required to survive, but also to ensure that one can live as a normative agent- conceiving and pursuing a worthwhile life. The minimum provision is that required to maintain life.

> "If human rights are protections of a form of life that is autonomous and free, they should protect that life as well as that form of it."[1]

This requires slightly more than just enough calories to stay alive, or just enough health that one is clinging to life, it requires that one has enough of the basics so that one is in a position to reflect and assess, not merely struggling to survive. This determination of minimum provision tends to approach Griffin's description of liberty. The means to be at liberty to pursue a conception of a worthwhile life include a minimum provision of basic necessities, otherwise one is not at liberty- one spends time scraping to survive. That this is one of the higher-order human rights of Griffin's theory runs counter to many theories of human rights.

Griffin also refers to minimum provision as *welfare*. The twentieth century was marked by a conflict between the obligations to provide welfare in various forms. Politics in many countries centre around the preferred approach to welfare- such as in the United States where one either supports a Republican view of freedom and a minimal state, or one favours a Democratic approach to increased welfare provision and the obligations that brings. In the United Kingdom more than a decade of Conservative rule has been followed by a decade of Labour, welfare centred politics, and it looks like the future will bring back a Conservative party to power as recession takes hold.

While the requirement remains less contentious under this substantive approach to human rights, welfare (minimum provision) is contested in libertarian approaches, where provision of welfare is viewed as forced labour.[2] Under Griffin's substantive approach, the level of welfare required is that which allows one to be an autonomous and free person. The level of autonomy and liberty required is that ill-defined threshold of normative agency. However, to add some clarity, Griffin refers to a case of famine

> "Food aid in a famine may do little to change that person's life. It may merely keep that person alive until the next famine. It is most unlikely that a person could rise to normative agency in such circumstances: no education, no leisure, no hope, no ambition, no long view. What such a person needs for normative agency is a remedy for these lacks."[3]

While providing for access to education and the basics of food and shelter, Griffin seems to be contending that minimum provision ought to provide enough time for leisure, for generating a long term view, a demanding obligation on society if one consider the state of the world, the huge number of people who do toil to survive, to merely provide for themselves and their family. However, Griffin does not consider this too onerous an obligation.

The Universal Declaration and the succeeding UN Covenant on Economic, Social and Cultural Rights provide the global legal basis for welfare rights. However, the moral rights of Griffin's theory and the UN documents do not easily reconcile themselves. While Griffin's theory is one of minimum provision, the UDHR in Article 25.1 for example, calls for

> "the right to a standard of living adequate for the health and well-being of himself and of his family, including food, clothing, housing and medical care and necessary social services, and the right to security in the event of unemployment, sickness, disability, widowhood, old age or other lack of livelihood in circumstances beyond his control."

The right to a standard of living adequate for health and well-being seems to be beyond the level of minimum provision proscribed by Griffin. Griffin, above, does call for a requirement of a certain amount of leisure, but it is implausible that 'periodic holidays with pay' as called for under Article 24 of the UDHR would conceivably fall under Griffins requirements for normative agency, indeterminate though it is. However, the right to minimum provision is not of immediate concern to this volume on the right to live a nomadic life, as will be discussed in later sections.

Griffin considers that autonomy, liberty and minimum provision are the three 'highest-level human rights'. The right to liberty, autonomy and minimum provision are universal human rights. All other human rights are derived from these and are essentially protections of our liberty, autonomy and minimum provision to the level of functioning as normative agents.[4] These we will refer to as 'second-order' human rights.

Summary

In this chapter I have attempted to develop a substantive account of how human rights can be derived and the content of the rights determined, considering James Griffin's theory of normative agency, being grounded in autonomy, liberty and minimum provision. Human rights are viewed as originating in the dignity of the human being, this dignity being that the human person acts as a normative agent: being able to conceive of, and pursue, a worthwhile life. The requirements of normative agency are liberty, autonomy and minimum provision. Human rights are protections of our status as a normative agent, requiring autonomy, liberty and minimum provision. When liberty is curtailed, normative agency is limited. When our autonomy is infringed, normative agency is reduced. Autonomy is limited by a lack of available choices, a lack of knowledge of these choices, or the mental capacities to determine second-order preferences. When welfare is lacking, the struggle for survival restricts autonomy and liberty. While these three 'higher order' human rights provide the basis for Griffin's theory, the three higher order rights tend to overlap. Griffin fails to determine what the threshold level of normative agency actually is and how it can be measured. This indeterminateness affects an interpretation of the three higher order human rights. The liberties that are considered to be worthy of protection by human rights remains unclear. Many rights that fall under the provision of creating an enabling environment for liberty seem to be minimum provision. There remains a blurring of the distinction between guaranteeing liberty to pursue a conception of worthwhile life, and facilitating success in achieving that conception. Regardless of the difficulties with the thesis, exploring a concrete example of a contested right, such as the right to live a nomadic life, will require engaging, examining and developing some of these inconsistencies. The next section will focus on the right to be nomadic and examine it within the boundaries of Griffin's conception of human rights as protectors of normative agency.

Part III:

The Right to be Nomadic

CHAPTER ELEVEN

LIBERTY, AUTONOMY AND MINIMUM PROVISION OF NOMADIC PERSONS

Nomadic groups, or members of groups with nomadic traditions, have a diverse range of lifestyles, backgrounds and personalities. Living a nomadic life can have different meanings to members of each group and to individual members within these groups. For individuals who are not members of such groups but who seek to break from a sedentary lifestyle and live a transient or peripatetic existence the existence of such a right may also be of importance.

The right to a nomadic lifestyle in an agrarian society, with seasonal climate change and harsher weather conditions may be determined by the right to minimum provision. Restricting the right of Bedouin nomads to move pasture when the season demands may render them unable to live an autonomous life as they are forced to struggle merely for survival, a condition that does not enable one to conceive of, and pursue, a worthwhile life. A nomadic life for the Saami in Sweden may be considered vital in maintaining their economic pursuits, in the absence of other options in a harsh Arctic climate. Indeed this right has been recognised as a transnational right in Scandinavia to allow herds of reindeer to be moved from climatic dependent pasture in one state to another. For members of the Travelling community, nomadism may be important in terms of earning a living.

> "It isn't just travelling for the sake of it, looking at the scenery; it is making a living, going to fairs and markets, hawking from door to door."[1]

Travelling for Irish Travellers has been a vital aspect of their way of life. Travellers, like business people, identify, and respond to, gaps in a market, providing particular services, in a particular manner- services in a manner that cannot be maintained by standard business models. Travelling may also be important in maintaining family bonds.

> "Your proudness links into your way of life, travelling, or being in a halting site or trailer or having your family or extended family around. Travellers would be stronger about their family."[2]

Traveller families, many of them large, extended family, congregate for extended periods in large groups, congregations that would be difficult to maintain as sedentary groups, whether spatially or economically. For some, Travelling is something that is linked to culture and tradition. A member of the Travelling community, in an interview at Pavee Point Traveller Centre in Dublin states:

> "There are other Travellers who are very strong about travelling. They don't give a damn. They want to keep a travelling way of life, around story-telling, keeping their language and traditions. My own grandfathers and mothers, they passed down information, and we can tell it to settled people, and pass it down to the next generation of Travellers, letting them know."[3]

Travelling is instrumental in maintaining culture, in passing on aspects of Traveller life that are valuable to members of the Travelling community in their own right. Without Travelling, maintaining Traveller language and traditions may be very difficult in competition with demands of adapting to sedentary society. The Irish language has struggled to survive in competition with the English language, the global language of commerce and education. Traditions of the Traveller community, including Traveller values, may be compromised or lost, if Travellers are not able to Travel and congregate in a particular manner. For others, Travelling is something more abstract and indefinable, with an intrinsic value.

> "There are some things you can't articulate. No matter who you are. You could be the most esteemed academic in the world in sociology or anthropology. Some things just can't be defined. It is all in the head. You just can't define it or articulate it. [Travelling] is there and it is important to you and that's ok. Not everything needs to be articulated you know."[4]

Travelling is important for what it is, for what it means to members of the Travelling community. There may be no instrumental or definable value; only the desire to travel, and the sense of 'something' that Travelling brings, whatever it is- a certain freedom, being on the road, moving from one place to another.

Human rights aim to protect the higher-order rights to autonomy, liberty and minimum provision which are necessary to live as a normative agent. Second-order rights are instrumental in the protection of these higher-order rights and are more specific derivations of these rights, whose content can be specific to times and places. Some of these circumstances can be the level of development of a society, the political and social situations within which members of a society exist, as well as the climate, the economic condition, availability of infrastructure etc.

The right to privacy is derived to protect the liberty and autonomy of individuals, to provide space for personal development, to not be interfered with arbitrarily. This right to privacy may be more relevant as we enter an era of increasingly invasive technologies, electronic monitoring etc., where governments can more easily invade the personal space of individuals. The right to freedom of expression leads to the right to freedom of the press in an increasingly complex and legalistic era, where independent media is necessary to ensure the maintenance of democracy. Freedom of the press may be necessary to avoid increasing propaganda which can limit the autonomy of the individual, in order to avoid a '1984' scenario. In the modern internet era, further rights (or controls) may be required to protect autonomy. In a society where the press does not exist, freedom of expression can be protected without requiring an independent media. The right to vote is dependent upon living in a liberal democratic society of representative democracy. A right to participation in decisions that affect one's circumstance is a necessary right to protect autonomy and liberty, and the right to vote is circumstantial to our particular societal structure. The right to vote may not be necessary in a consensual tribal village, where decisions are made based on reaching a consensus rather than majority decision making. In this manner, the universality of certain rights comes to be questioned, as certain derived rights, such as the right to a free press, are ahistorical and are contingent on a particular social construct. However, these derived rights are protections of autonomy, liberty and minimum provision, requirements for normative agency, and it is the protections that these derived right provide, that give them the status of human rights.

Examining the right to live a nomadic life and the content of the right may be contingent on the prevailing social and economic conditions. The grounding of the right exists in the protection of the autonomy, liberty and minimum provision of the individual to be a *normative agent*. This volume has already noted the difficulties around the lack of definition of a threshold of normative agency, below which human rights are required to protect a person from falling, and to enable each member of the human species to achieve. The succeeding sections of this chapter focus on nomadism in the context of a developed, liberal democratic society, such as those often referred to as the 'first world' or 'developed world'. Though it is impossible to generalize for all different groups of nomadic tradition, or indeed members of these groups, the chapter will refer to, and can be considered relevant to, the requirements of members of the Irish Traveller community and to Roma/Gypsy groups in Europe. The examination of nomadism as a right, will attempt to address some of the indeterminateness in this theory of human rights, with respect to liberty and autonomy. This volume will hopefully overcome the indeterminateness, without addressing the inherent difficulties that have been pointed out regarding liberty in pursuit of a worthwhile life, as opposed to actual fulfilment.

CHAPTER TWELVE

NOMADISM AND MINIMUM PROVISION

For the Irish Traveller and members of the Roma/Gypsy community, nomadism has historically been both an economic and social choice. Liegeois describes the role nomadism has played for Travellers in recent history

> "Nomadism is thus partly *structural*, arising from a certain type of social and economic organization and a desire for travel, and partly *reactive* to developments determined by others, such as measures of exclusion (eviction, deportation…) or containment (slavery, imprisonment, various prohibitions…). As a general rule both types of factors play a role in the decision to move on."[1]

For members of the Roma community, Travelling has historically been necessary for survival, not just for survival of the group and the group's identity, but for survival of individuals. Though the origins of the Roma/Gypsy Travellers remain contested, consensus is that the group entered Europe in the 13th century coming from north-western India, possibly as a result of upheavals in the area. The movement was precipitated by a need survive. Travelling for the Roma community has been a means to earning a living, but also a means to survive, as in many areas they were subject to violence in many forms, threats to the individual, and to the group. In some areas, Gypsies were forced to move on in areas where simply being a Gypsy was a crime. Travelling from town to town was necessary to earn a living in a time dominated by feudal landlords.

While minimum provision is instrumental in protecting normative agency, a nomadic lifestyle has been instrumental in ensuring that Travellers have been able to provide for themselves; to maintain minimum provision.[2] Travelling is an economic issue as well as a lifestyle choice. The right to minimum provision would seem to include the right to maintain a travelling lifestyle, as Travelling is required for survival.

Travelling is instrumental to providing shelter and income for the basics in life, such as food, health and education.

However, though travelling is instrumental, it is not a necessary condition, for minimum provision. The requirement for minimum provision can be, and is, met for members of the group who choose to, or have been forced to, whether by direct governmental coercion, or by economic necessity, sedentarise. In many cases, sedentarisation is in fact a more suitable lifestyle choice, in order to maintain minimum provision, as a sedentary-oriented societal structure has made maintaining an economically viable Travelling lifestyle more difficult and less worthwhile than a sedentarised, subsidised life.

> "So, Gypsies who have maintained their traditional itinerant lifestyle are faced with the following dilemma. They can either opt for stability and integration into the sedentary world in order to qualify for social assistance, rent relief, proper schooling, etc, but at the price of giving up their mobility and, with it, many of the available opportunities for earning a living; or they can maintain their old way of life at the price of losing their social, and often political rights (voting, participating in public life), because they are largely incompatible with such mobility."[3]

A sedentarised lifestyle provides improved access to health, welfare benefits, education, running water, sanitation than is available at present, in societies that are geared toward sedentarised living. The argument for minimum provision, as a protection of normative agency, is not strong enough to require a right for members of groups who have a preference for a nomadic lifestyle, no more than any other individual has a *human* right to employment in a particular profession of preference. Though, it can be argued that as the state facilitates provision of these services for settled communities, fairness or equality may require that both lifestyle choices be supported in the same manner. However, based on the justification of a protection of normative agency through minimum provision, nomadism is not a human right.[4]

CHAPTER THIRTEEN

NOMADISM AND LIBERTY

Liberty, as a function of normative agency, is the freedom in the pursuit of one's consideration of a worthwhile life. Many Irish Travellers and Roma/Gypsy nomads have sedentarised, and no longer wish to pursue a transient lifestyle. However, many members of these groups continue to attempt to do so. For the Irish Traveller the freedom to pursue this lifestyle has been restricted by the Housing (Miscellaneous Provisions) Act of 2002 and the failure of Local Authorities to provide transient sites for Travellers as proposed under the Traveller Accommodation Act of 1998. Donahue, McVeigh & Ward quote a Traveller woman from Westmeath who outlines the effect of the 2002 Act, and, how some members of the Travelling community continue to risk imprisonment by maintaining a way of life that is pushed to the margins in society.

> "It has affected Travellers in a very bad way – it has taken away their culture from them. All the camps are blocked up. They don't have the freedom to travel – that freedom has been taken off them. Who has the right to do that to anyone? There's some of them doing it anyway. They are charged, they are fined, they are getting their caravans taken off them. They are left homeless because of the law. (Younger Woman: Tullamore)"[1]

Members of the Travelling community continue to live a travelling lifestyle despite the restrictions imposed under the 2002 Act, and the failure of local government to provide transient accommodation to the level required by the Travelling community under the 1998 Act. As a result, Travellers are criminalised by their actions, and they are labelled as criminals by society, though the fairness of the legislation is obviously under question in this volume. As a result, whether through statistics or through the presence of Gardaí on encampments which are now unlawful, Travellers are increasingly viewed as criminal. Reporting of these statistics, with trespass as a criminal offence, creates, and propagates, the impression of Travellers as criminal. Irrespective of the other criminal offences that are committed by society, or by Travellers, criminalising trespass has the effect of skewing crime statistics against those who travel as part of their way of life.

Chapter 1 has shown that legislation in Ireland effectively criminalizes Travellers who continue to move. Travelling is rendered virtually impossible through the Roads Act, the 2002 Housing Act and the failure of the Local Authorities to provide for Traveller Accommodation under the 1998 Act. The 2002 Act has altered trespass from being a tort to being a criminal offence. Increased powers for the Gardaí mean that the Traveller home can be confiscated and custodial sentences imposed, through a law that is not clearly defined. Where a Traveller person risks living a nomadic life, he lives with the very real risk of arbitrary arrest, based on a 'possibility' of a 'likelihood' of such ill-defined terms as 'interfering', 'substantially' and 'damaging', should they place a transit vehicle, a home, outside of defined transient accommodation.

Human rights as a protection of normative agency require the freedom to pursue conceptions of a worthwhile life. For Travellers, maintaining a nomadic lifestyle is a conception of what constitutes a worthwhile life.

> "Nomadism entails a way of looking at the world, a different way of perceiving things, a different attitude to accommodation, to work, and to life in general."[2]

For Travellers, nomadism is more than simply a lifestyle choice; it involves a way of life that is valuable intrinsically to the Traveller. It involves the freedom to choose a particular aspect of life that is part of an outlook on life different to that of the sedentary population.

> "Country people organize every aspect of their lives- from neighbourhood watch to parishes to electoral constituencies- in the fact of sedentarism, the fact that they live permanently side-by-side with a fixed group of other people. Travellers, on the other hand, organize every aspect of their lives around family ties; The Traveller's very identity requires 'keeping in touch', and this in turn requires travel."[3]

For those who live a sedentary lifestyle, it may be difficult to understand, or relate to, the value of a Travelling life. It may be that many of us are accustomed to, and oriented toward, sedentary living, that the values that accompany living outside this rubric are difficult to comprehend. In a globalised world, where individuals are becoming increasingly atomised, a way of life that is oriented around physically 'keeping in touch' is incomprehensible to many. With modern 'electronic' communication, and a shrinking world where physical interaction is becoming increasingly sacrificed in favour of virtual relationships, communal and communitarian tendencies seem to be increasingly out of place. With emphasis on maintaining a sense of community with an extended family, the Traveller way of life is increasingly at odds with sedentary society.

The freedom to pursue a way of life which includes nomadism is valuable for the Traveller as it forms part of how the Traveller views the world. Though society in general is organised to facilitate a sedentary mindset- a different outlook on life- human rights under normative agency should protect the liberty of the Traveller to pursue a nomadic way of life. Human rights, under Griffin's substantive approach, are not a guarantee of a flourishing life. The right to live a nomadic life is not a right that should guarantee a flourishing nomadic life, but a right to the liberty to pursue this lifestyle. The right would require that the pursuit of this lifestyle not be denied. Legislation enacted in Ireland directly interferes with this freedom and restricts it to the extent that it is impossible to live a nomadic life without being labelled a criminal. However, in a society such as Ireland, a simple liberty right would fail to provide the freedom to live a nomadic life, as sedentarised society has co-opted the availability of land to facilitate sedentary living, rendering the possibility of a transient lifestyle increasingly difficult.

Niner highlights how sedentary society dominates to such an extent that it provides transient sites for members of sedentary society for recreational activity, while restricting transience for those of whom it is a valuable way of life.

> "While the task [of providing transient accommodation] seems large relative to current transit site provision, comparison with the number of camping and caravan sites available to the settled population for holiday purposes puts it into perspective. For example, the Caravan Club (just one among several organisations) has over 200 club sites and 2700 'certified locations', small sites for no more than five caravans with varying levels of service provision (Caravan Club, 2003), much more than might be required for Gypsies and Travellers."[4]

It seems ironic that Traveller lifestyle is restricted, while society facilitates recreational travelling, which is oriented toward sedentary society. Spatial distribution provides for commercially oriented recreational travel, while restricting commercial travel for those that it is an economic requirement, and a desired way of life. Temporary travelling, when one is oriented in a sedentary mode of living, is acceptable and facilitated under a market-driven demand. At the same time, society no longer provides space for a Travelling life that is viewed as having outlived the market's requirement.

As a member of the Bray Traveller Community Development Group states, the aim of Traveller Organisations is to push for the establishment of a network of transient halting sites around Ireland

> "to try and implement the transit halting sites, to try and bring back some sort of nomadism within the Travelling communities and they have the right to say if there is a travelling site down in Clare and it's a pull in and pull out site, and all the structures have to be there, if I go down for three months, pay my little bit of rent, I have electricity and water, go there for three months and move back up to my house."[5]

The freedom to live a nomadic lifestyle is outlined under a plan of spatial orientation, requiring a relatively small area of the spatial distribution to be allocated to a Traveller way of life, with basic services provided.

The idea that improved welfare, plus access to health and education for Travellers, can only be achieved by sedentarisation is a policy that has been attempted in many countries in recent history. It is a policy which has led to the sedentarisation of members of many nomadic groups, but at great cost to many members of the groups, and to the group identity itself. Bancroft highlights various other approaches taken by States to induce sedentarisation.

> "Similarly, instances of state sanctioned kidnap or Roma and Gypsy-Traveller children were defended as for the child's own good. The countries which operated these policies ranged from the progressive welfare states of Scandinavia to the eliminationist social engineering state of Nazi Germany."[6]

While the motivation for the various policies in dealing with Roma and Gypsy Travellers may have been different, the outcomes of the policies have rarely been positive, when viewed from the perspective of the Traveller groups. Bancroft also indicts the Swiss, Irish, Norwegian, British, Czech and Hungarian states.

> "The control of children by the state was instituted to deal with what was viewed as the primary delinquency of Gypsies, their nomadic lifestyle."[7]

Restriction of the liberty to be nomadic was enacted under the guise of child welfare- removing children from what was viewed as a 'bad' way of life, away from the families, into a 'better' future in sedentarised society. In Ireland, this process of sedentarisation began in 1963.

> "The state began to intervene in this context for the first time with the *Commission on Itinerancy* which reported in 1963. This marked the beginning of an explicit *settlement policy* – in which the state encouraged Travellers to abandon nomadism and 'assimilate' into sedentary Irish society."[8]

The terms of reference given to the Commission on Itinerancy required it:

> "(1) to enquire into the problem arising from the presence in the country of itinerants in considerable numbers;
> (2) to examine the economic, educational, health and social problems inherent in their way of life;
> (3) to consider what steps might be taken –
>   (a) to provide opportunities for a better way of life for itinerants;
>   (b) to promote their absorption into the general community;
>   (c) pending such absorption, to reduce to a minimum the disadvantages to themselves and to the community resulting from their itinerant habits;
>   (d) to improve the position generally; and
> (4) to make recommendations."[9]

At its inception, the language in the terms of reference presented the Commission with a partisan task. The Commission was required to delve into the problem of Traveller groups, arising from their presence in and around residential areas. Any problems associated with Travellers in relation to health, education or social issues were to be viewed as inherent in their way of life. It was not considered that the problems in Traveller life could be related to the interaction with sedentary society, or caused by sedentary society. The aim was to promote absorption of the Traveller community into society as the pre-determined solution- it was only a matter of figuring out how best to do this. Any disadvantage was assumed to be due to Traveller 'habits', a disparaging view of the chosen way of life of the Traveller. The approach failed to address the possibility of disadvantage being due to the failure of sedentary society to accommodate for Traveller lifestyle. The attitude toward Travelling was reaffirmed by then Minister for Justice, Charles J. Haughey, stating

> "These terms of reference are comprehensive and they acknowledge that there can be no final solution to the problems created by itinerants until they are absorbed into the general community."[10]

This was to be the approach followed by the Irish State in finding a *final solution* to the 'Itinerant problem' for the next 35 years. Throughout this time, relations between settled and Traveller communities were topical as settled communities struggled to remove Traveller encampments from their areas. As an unofficial boulder policy was used by many Local Authorities to prevent Travellers stopping in seasonal encampments, Travellers struggled to gain access to services. Policies adopted of preventing Travellers from returning to traditional stopping sites encouraged the growth of large-scale Traveller encampments, usually in sites lacking adequate services such as water and sanitation, situation in unappealing and often, unsanitary locations. Local community antipathy toward Travellers was compounded and animated by the growth of such encampments, and the associated social problems that accompanied these. Travellers gradually realised that they had to become engaged in order to protect the interests of their community, and raise Traveller issues at a political and national level. In official discourse the problem was never described in such terms as a conflict of spatial control, ideology, or simply, control.

> "Traveller nomadism is the very antithesis of such sedentary notions of 'fixed abode'. Travellers are never 'from somewhere' in this sense – they are coming from somewhere and going somewhere else."[11]

The problem was never addressed as one where two modes of living came clashed. Sedentary society requires certain controls and regulations and is based on each individual having a fixed abode. Travellers, historically, tended to be between abodes. In increasingly centralised and regulated societies, societies with citizenship, and responsibilities, the problem of a group of people that didn't fit into this model needed to be solved.

The enacting of the Traveller Accommodation Act seemed to be an acceptance that paternalistic policies of doing what was in the *interest* of Travellers had failed amidst the resistance of many members of the Travelling community to settle, despite harsh conditions characterized by lack of clean running water, poor sanitation and general hostility to nomadism. However, just prior to this, the Governmental Task Force on the Travelling Community (1995) reported

> "Nomadism in the context to today's traveller lifestyle is a contentious and emotive issue but any lifestyle which places that community at a significant disadvantage in virtually every walk of life and which is inordinately expensive on the taxpaying community to maintain for the questionable benefit of a small section of the population must be regularly reviewed in the interest of society as a whole and *particularly in the interests of that community.*"(my emphasis)[12]

The impression given by the Task Force is that a Travelling lifestyle is inordinately expensive on the tax-paying community, and that Travelling places the community at a "significant disadvantage" relative to sedentary populations. The insinuation that supporting a Traveller lifestyle is not only expensive, but inordinately expensive is contentious to say the least, and arguably false. The associated costs with rendering nomadism virtually impossible are possibly greater than the costs of facilitating a Traveller lifestyle. The potential benefits of providing, and legitimising Travelling, rather than criminalising Travelling provide an economic argument, which benefits society as a whole and the Travelling community in particular. The assumption again, lacking in-depth investigation, is that nomadism is the cause of disadvantage, rather than society's marginalisation of nomadism, contrary to the acceptance and promotion of sedentarism.

The Report highlighted that the State continues to play a role in seeking to determine what a worthwhile life is for the Travelling community in spite of Traveller resistance showing that nomadism is more than simply a casual lifestyle choice. Bancroft encapsulated the clash between the British State and Travellers there.

> "There seems to be a cycle in the spatial relationships between the British State and the Gypsy-Travellers, with the state asserting methods of spatial control and then Gypsy-Travellers finding ways to subvert it."[13]

Such is the desire of the Traveller to maintain the connection with a transient life that repeated assertions of control by the State are resisted. It is a mark of Traveller culture, being such a small minority in many states, their interests regularly subsumed beneath those of sedentary society, that rather than engage in an impossible conflict, the approach is one of subversion. Gypsy-Travellers have historically engaged in a type of 'guerrilla lawfare'. Removed from political interaction, but seeking to survive as a nomadic group, legislation was rarely challenged, but its implementation subverted by the Travellers seeking to travel in spite of the law.

Griffin's idea of liberty as a function of normative agency remains indeterminate. However, for the liberty to pursue particular lifestyle choices to be protected by human rights, these choices have to be particularly valuable. Griffin's theory does not clearly spell out any formula for determining how to evaluate the 'value' of the required liberty. The right to smoke a cigarette or to go to the cinema everyday would not fall under the guise of human rights as the liberty to do these would not be considered important enough. It would be reasonably safe to assert that one would remain a normative agent even of one cannot go to the cinema. One would hardly fall beneath that ill-defined threshold. It is not so clear-cut when we consider the liberty to pursue a nomadic life. The liberty to pursue a lifestyle (nomadism) that

> "entails a way of looking at the world, a different way of perceiving things, a different attitude to accommodation, to work, and to life in general"

would seem to require a strong protection; a protection that conceivably falls under human rights. This would require that the right to be nomadic be a 'trump' on the aim of sedentary society to manage spatial distribution in a manner that promotes private property and permanent residence, though supporting nomadism is perceived to be

> "inordinately expensive on the taxpaying community to maintain for the questionable benefit of a small section."[14]

A member of the Travelling community outlines what is required to facilitate the pursuit of a nomadic life:

> "What we need is a network of halting sites, so therefore there is nothing stopping me, not just for 3 months, but what about 6 months, I have been in Wexford for three months, what's stopping me going from Wexford to Waterford, like we used to when I was young, where there is another halting site, if it was properly structured and serviced, its not rocket science we are talking about, it can be achieved, and for a small sum of money."[15]

The notion that facilitating Transient lifestyles is inordinately expensive is contested and the costs of resulting from restricting nomadism may outweigh the savings made in failing to provide a network of serviced transient sites for Travellers.

> "There exists therefore widespread concern, not only about the amount of money and other resources expended on unauthorised encampments, but also as to the wisdom of such expenditure. Paradoxically, while the current policy relating to accommodation for Travelling People was originally informed about the costs of site provision, no research had been conducted concerning the costs of non-provision of authorised and appropriate sites."[16]

The costs of non-provision are related to areas such as education, the costs for cleaning and maintaining sites, legal and court costs, as well as police costs, of evictions the cost for the health services directly related to non-provision of suitable Traveller accommodation to mention a few.

While a paternalistic state may seek to regulate lifestyles to suit the rational choices of normative agents, there remains a question as to what constitutes rationality. What seems irrational and impenetrable from one perspective may be common sense from another. The historic experiences of Roma, Gypsy/Travellers of sedentarised life in Europe may lead these groups to continue to view a nomadic lifestyle as rational. Assimilation and integration have been associated with sedentarisation in the past, and nomadism has often been a means to avoid submission to societies which continue to marginalize the nomad. Recent histories include forced settlement of Gypsies, sterilization, forced removal of Traveller children and the *porrajmos*, where approximately half a million Gypsies died in the Holocaust.[17]

> "It is the case that Roma and Gypsy-Traveller often describe gauje (settled) behaviour in precisely these terms, as impenetrable and irrational."[18]

Bancroft describes different types of rationalities that may be significant in Roma and Gypsy-Travellers choosing alternative lifestyles. These are economic rationalities, bureaucratic rationality, substantive and formal rationalities in law, and minority counter-rationalities.[19]

It seems anathema to the idea of liberty to place restrictions on a mode of living that is intrinsically valuable to members of a particular group, when human rights are viewed in a substantive manner as being protections of our status as normative agents. Humans cease to be normative agents when there is no longer liberty, autonomy or minimum provision. The level of these three requirements to reach the undefined level of normative agents remains indeterminate, yet, when liberty consists of pursuing conceptions of a worthwhile life, and Travellers have a strong sense that Travelling is a significant portion of their conception of a worthwhile life, then denial of the right to be nomadic seems to be an infringement of the higher level right to liberty.

The next section will examine the right to be nomadic as a function of the higher level right to autonomy, as a requirement of normative agency. The value of liberty to pursue a nomadic life will be examined as a protection of the third of the higher-level human rights, the autonomy of the individual. Rather than nomadism being merely an extravagant personal whim, the argument based on autonomy aims to show that this right to pursue a nomadic life is intrinsically and instrumentally valuable, and denial of such has severe impacts on the autonomy of the individual.[20] The right to be nomadic is intrinsically valuable to the Traveller identity, and instrumentally valuable in protecting the autonomy of the Traveller.

Earlier problems concerning Griffin's thesis of human rights, as protections of our status as normative agents, centred on the indeterminateness of the threshold of normative agency. It is not clear when one falls below this threshold. As normative agency is comprised of liberty, autonomy and minimum provision, it is these three factors, either singly or in combination, are denied, that agency is affected. Liberty to pursue a conception of a worthwhile life is the liberty in question. It is not clear when liberty to pursue becomes a liberty to achieve, or liberty to succeed. However, also in question is which pursuits are important enough to require the protection of human rights? In attempting to solve this dilemma, the next section will look at the effects of the denial of this liberty on the autonomy of members of the Traveller community. Liberty to pursue a nomadic life is viewed as important enough to require the protection of human rights, if, when this liberty is denied, autonomy is infringed. Determining when this liberty to pursue a conception of worthwhile life becomes liberty to succeed is also dependant on the effects on autonomy of the individual; when the ability to conceive of alternative versions of a worthwhile life is impaired.

CHAPTER FOURTEEN

NOMADISM AND AUTONOMY

The requirement that human rights protect autonomy as a function of normative agency is the third of the three *high-level* rights to be considered. Autonomy as part of normative agency is the ability to conceive of a worthwhile life. How do we know when a person becomes autonomous, or when autonomy is restricted in such a manner as to require the protection of human rights? This is a question that is very difficult and contested, and requires more than simple assertion. There are three aspects to autonomy; the first is that there are alternative versions of what may be considered a worthwhile life available, the second is having knowledge of this array of options which can be considered, and the third is having the mental capacities to understand and choose these options.

Autonomy seems to focus on being able to identify options for a worthwhile life while liberty involves being able to pursue these. However, if these options are not viable or real, then autonomy is restricted. If one cannot avail of the option to be nomadic can it be considered as a real option? For one member of the Travelling community, whether there is a current desire to travel or not, is not the issue.

> "It's about having the right. I remember doing a presentation in a secondary school a couple of years ago. I remember one of the pupils, secondary school, said to me about pubs and discrimination, 'Do you drink?' and at the time I didn't drink a huge amount. He said 'Well if you don't drink why do you need the pubs?' They completely missed the point. It's irrelevant whether I drink or not. What's relevant is that if I want to go into a pub and have a drink if I so wish, I can. Whether it is alcohol or a mineral or whatever, it's a right and about me having the right to exercise that right. It doesn't really matter how many Travellers will travel, when they will travel, how they will travel, it's about having that right respected and whether the state will put the policies in place to allow that right, resource and facilities. Whether I travel or not in the next 20 years is not the point."[1]

It seems that autonomy requires knowledge of the existence of different conceptions of life, that these are truly available and the mental ability or capacity to choose between the options. The freedom to pursue these conceptions only comes into play once an option has been conceived as worthwhile. To be autonomous, one needs to have an available array of options and knowledge of these in order to make first order preferences. Also, one needs to have the mental capacity to assess and review these first order preferences- that is, to make second order preferences.[2]

However, normative agency does not require that the available array of options be limitless. It is not clear how many options constitute a rich array of options. Nor is it definitive as to which options are considered important enough to be considered to fall under the protection of human rights. Certain human rights, such as the right to participate in a democratic society are closely linked to autonomy, as it allows the individual to have a say in decisions that affect that person. Slavery and torture are anathema to autonomy. Torture is carried out to eliminate the personhood of the individual, to prevent the person from thinking autonomously. Slavery is about domination. Slavery takes away choice. This is why protection from slavery and torture are the first things we think of when we talk of human rights.

Are there other rights that are required to protect autonomy? One's autonomy is infringed if one is indoctrinated in such a manner that it does not allow one to assess the first order preferences, or if there are no real first order preferences. If one does not have comparative choices to make as to what constitutes a worthwhile life one's autonomy is restricted. One's autonomy is infringed if one is subject to propaganda and brain-washing. Autonomy seems to be about retaining the ability to critically think, review and assess one's options. Yet, this does not tell us which options are necessary to constitute protecting. It is difficult to determine which options are important enough. One may claim that one's autonomy is infringed if cars are available "in every colour, so long as it's black", yet this clearly does not fall under the protection of human rights. It isn't sufficiently important. Lindley, regarding autonomy, states that:

> "One is not seeking to deny people the freedom to take decisions which appear to (and may actually) be against their interests, provided the decision is not taken in ignorance."[3]

Liberal democracies seek not to determine what a conception of the good life is, but to allow the freedom to determine for oneself, which requires autonomy. Lindley goes further stating that restricting the availability of options limits the development of autonomy.

> "Autonomy develops only in those who are allowed to practice making their own decisions, even when such decisions may be unwise."[4]

Is nomadism sufficiently important to require the protection of human rights? Is it necessary to have the option to choose between a sedentary and a peripatetic lifestyle? For members of groups that have traditionally maintained a nomadic lifestyle, it seems that this may be true. Nomadism is important in maintaining traditional family bonds, economic lifestyle, maintenance of culture and retaining a separate language. For members of sedentary society it may not be of such importance. How do we weigh up the importance of having such a choice? It is necessary to return to Griffin's circularity that it falls under the protection of human rights if it is required to protect normative agency, that facet that we find so valuable in the human person. We are only normative agents if we can conceive of and pursue an idea of a worthwhile life, whatever that may be.

The argument regarding autonomy and nomadism seems to be at an impasse. While an available array of options is necessary, and it seems that nomadism is an important option for Travellers, it is difficult to determine whether it is important enough to fall under the protection of human rights. The only way to approach a solution is to request the assistance of anthropologists and to examine research in the area on the effects of limiting or restricting the option of leading a nomadic lifestyle on those it affects. There has been little research carried out in the area of the impact of sedentarisation, or restricting nomadic movement. However, it is difficult to ascertain whether the effects are due to sedentarisation itself, or to ancillary effects that accompany sedentarisation, such as the attitudes of the settled community to Travellers/Gypsies who settle in the area, the effects of ghettoisation, poor employment and education availability, or educational systems that are not inclusive of Traveller/Gypsy families and end up alienating and creating further social problems.

The question requiring an answer is whether the restriction of nomadism prevents one from being able to conceive of *a* worthwhile life- does restricting one's particular preference of his/her worthwhile life (transience/nomadism), restrict the ability to conceive of *a* worthwhile life- that is, to determine second order preferences? Jean-Pierre Liegeois has carried out considerable research into Roma and Gypsy communities for the Council of Europe and draws some conclusions regarding the impact of sedentarisation. These consist of the more obvious direct impacts on health and earning capacity.

> "Among the side effects are a rise in health problems (sometimes termed 'the pathology of sedentarisation') and financial ones (sedentary living entails a number of additional expenses but reduces earning capacity)...

Yet, the impact of sedentarisation is beneath the surface as well, and manifests itself in aberrant behaviour.

> ...The persistent dream of travel, when it can no longer be fulfilled, brings dissatisfaction, maladaptation, and aggression, which in turn can lead to delinquency, run-ins with the law, and a resulting stigmatization exacerbating the group's marginalism.

On another level, the sub-surface malaise is manifesting itself in terms of more complex psycho-social constructs.

> ...Indications of even deeper malaise are currently appearing, symptoms of desperation: drug abuse among some young people, hypochondria and over-medication, alcohol abuse, family destructuration; even the unprecedented phenomenon of child abandonment has occurred, though sometimes little choice has been involved (for example where pogroms have left Gypsy families homeless, illness and harsh weather conditions have forced them to put their children into care)."[5]

Liegeois highlights a number of different effects of sedentarisation. While the financial difficulties associated with sedentarisation may be remedied by appropriate welfare schemes, it is not clear whether remedies can be found to some of the other effects of sedentarisation, without provision of the liberty to live a nomadic life. The 'pathology of sedentarisation' is evident in Europe among Roma and Gypsy-Travellers. Health problems are not necessarily physical, but psychological, or psycho-somatic. Other pathologies are maladaptation, aggressions and dissatisfaction. These effects impinge on the mental capacities to form second order preferences. Further, the pathologies arising from sedentarisation may be symptomatic of the effects on the autonomy of members of the group, as a result of sedentarisation. The malaise and disillusionment due to sedentarisation- either directly or indirectly- results in substance abuse and hypochondria, further impacting on autonomy.

While further rigorous research into the issue is surely required, it seems that the effects on individual members of groups when nomadism is denied, leads to strong consideration for the right to be nomadic as a protection of autonomy. One research report into suicide among members of the Traveller community highlights the potential negative effects of sedentarisation.

> "Living in a house may even cause adverse psychological effects, including isolation, loneliness, loss of identity and feelings of being closed in (Ginnety, 1993 cited in Heron et al., 2000:109). Once in standard housing there is little hope of their being accommodated on a halting site (ITM, 2002a:10)"[6]

Though many of the side effects of sedentarisation outlined above may seem like personal choices, it is required to assess whether this is in fact the case.[7] The actions of members of the group, if they are a direct result of sedentarisation, resulting in depression, desperation, drug abuse, where this may not happen had the option of leading a nomadic lifestyle remained open, must be considered as infringements into the autonomy of individuals. Bancroft highlights some examples of the impact of sedentarisation on members of the Travelling community.

> "Many previously nomadic Gypsy-Travellers have to cope with very real problems when moving into housing, some psychological, some sociological. Feelings of depression and isolation are common…"[8]

These are not assumptions. Bancroft includes some notes from conversations which bear witness to the difficulties encountered by members of Travelling communities upon settling.

> "Penny, Voluntary Sector Worker, 1998 'They get into the house, feel imprisoned, don't get on with neighbours. It's a very isolating environment'."[9]

> "Nick- Scottish Traveller, 1998 'When I'm in the house I just sit by the fire all day. I feel like I'm dying, dying of boredom. There's no one to speak to, nothing to do. In a trailer, there's less space, but then that doesn't bother me. That's where I am happiest. I was born in a trailer'."[10]

These professions indicate a malaise, and are backed up by statistical data that shows that nomadic groups are a subordinated group in society. When Travellers are sedentarised they remain at the margins of society. Access to education, health (morbidity and mortality), life expectancy, and maternal health data, all show that Travellers continue to live at the periphery.

Just as a consumer may lose freedom of choice due to propaganda and incessant positive advertising, it is conceivable that the removal of a lifestyle choice can lead to individuals, due to depression, desperation or a sense of hopelessness, to feel there is no choice, and the only solution is, for example, a first-order preference for anti-social behaviour, alcohol or drug consumption. Whether, directly or indirectly, it is plausible that sedentarisation is having this effect on members of the Travelling community. Anecdotal evidence is pointing in this direction.

Autonomy involves second order preferences, and when an individual is no longer able to form second order preferences then autonomy has been infringed. Autonomy requires the protection of human rights. Depression, addictions and schizophrenia have been cited as restrictions in determining second order preferences, a list that is not exhaustive. The effects of sedentarisation have been shown to lead to some of the psychological problems outlined above, though research and correlation of data is currently lacking.

During conversations with a representative of the Travelling community, in response to whether the interviewee had witnessed in seven years, an increase in social and psychological problems among Travellers since the enacting of the 2002 Housing (Miscellaneous Provisions) Act.

> "Yes, tragically would say there has been an increase in suicide among the Travelling community, there is a book by Mary Rose Walker, in a section of her book she blames the lack of progress in service provision. Just about depression in younger Travellers, its harder to get accommodation when you get married, if you are going to be stuck in a home that is overcrowded, on top of your father and mother, that's not a tradition in the Travelling community. That's exactly what we are seeing among younger Travellers, some are even taking up drugs and alcohol. Now alcohol has always been there as a problem in the Travelling community, but hey, Ireland itself has a big alcohol problem. A lot of places are psychological problems, and sadly, we can say it out in the open, where does it lead from, it leads form all we are talking about, we haven't got that choice anymore, that choice has been taken and robbed from us by the powers that be."[11]

While the impact of sedentarisation on members of the Travelling community seems to have more negative than positive effects, restrictions on autonomy are not limited to the type of clinical psychological determinants outlined above. Autonomy is also vulnerable to intersubjective elements based on interaction with individuals and society in general. The legal and social mis-recognition of nomadism plays a role in curtailing the autonomy of members of the Travelling community.

In the next section, the idea of recognition among individuals in society, and among societal groups, will be examined. This will focus around Honneth's *Struggle for Recognition* and the impact of mis-recognition on autonomy, with regard to self-confidence, self-respect and self-esteem. The latter part of the section will examine nomadism and the aspect of mutual recognition between sedentary society and nomadic groups.

Chapter Fifteen

Nomadism, Autonomy, Recognition and Oppression

In the final section of this chapter, I explore how the autonomy of the individual is connected to recognition of one's way of life. More precisely, in the case of peripatetic groups and Irish Traveller, the lack of recognition of nomadism as a viable and socially acceptable way of life, and the associated oppression of Roma & Gypsy/Travellers, leads to the erosion of the autonomy of members of the Travelling community. Sedentary society tends to view the actions of members of the Travelling community as outside of societally acceptable behaviour. While not condoning any particular behaviour of individuals analysing the acceptability of actions of individuals must be placed in context. The first context is that behaviour of non-sedentary groups takes place within a framework oriented toward and designed by sedentary society. That these actions seem out-of-step with society may be due to the fact that society is simply arranged to make it seem so. Secondly, sedentary-oriented society has created laws to arrange society in a manner that fits sedentary living, and modes of living that seek to exist outside the model of the majority society, will be at risk of falling outside the law. Further, and as this section will attempt to show, the actions of peripatetic society can be related to a lack of recognition given to a mode of living, and people that follow that lifestyle, caused by the fact that society is oriented toward a lifestyle contrary to nomadism. This lack of recognition, both socially and legally, affects self-esteem, self-respect and self-confidence of members of transient groups. The reduction in these three intersubjective elements impinges on the autonomy of the individual, and thus, normative agency.

Iris Marion Young, in her seminal essay on 'Polity and Group Difference'[1] identifies a social group as

> "Involv[ing] first of all an affinity with other persons by which they identify with one another, and by which other people identify them. A person's particular sense of history, understanding of social relations and

personal possibilities, her or his mode of reasoning, values, and expressive styles are constituted at least partly by her or his group identity."[2]

Rather than entering into a discussion of whether Traveller's or Roma/Gypsies are an ethnic, cultural or national minority, for the purpose of this section their identification as a 'social group' is less contentious. Taking Young's conception of a social group, Travellers can be identified as such given that members of the group identify with a particular outlook on life; they identify with each other, and are identified as such by wider society. They have a particular sense of history, separate to that of Irish society, contested though it may be. And Travellers as a group do have a particular sense of social relations, a communitarian view of group relations, with particular social norms, customs and traditions, many of which are intrinsically associated with nomadism, and nomadism is instrumentally important in maintaining them. The Task Force identified that:

> "visible markers of Traveller culture include Traveller nomadism, the importance of the extended family, the Traveller language and the organisation of the Traveller economy."[3]

justifying their classification as a distinct social group. O' Reilly elaborates the markers that delineate the distinction between Travellers and 'sedentary people'.

> "Numerous contrasts can be made between the two lifestyles. Sedentary people see themselves as employees, while Travellers see themselves as self-employed. Sedentary people depend on a single trade or industry while Travellers depend on diversified occupations. Sedentary society is based on capital-intensive technology, while Travellers' society is based on labour. Sedentary people work individually away from the family while in Travellers' society the family is often involved in production. Sedentary people have a specific work/leisure division of hours, days weeks and have set holidays, while Travellers have no work leisure division- time-off is a personal choice and there are no set holidays. In sedentary society, orders are issued from above and there is usually a fixed routine, while Travellers impose their own orders and decisions, and routine is self-structured. In sedentary society training and education take place in institutions external to the family while in Travellers society training and education were traditionally based in the family. Sedentary society is based on payment of wages, while Travellers' society is based on individually negotiated profits."[4]

Travellers in Ireland are also externally identified as a social group, and Travellers, whether sedentary or transient, are identified by the 'settled' community as separate and distinct. A report into attitudes of settled people identified this separateness. They are not a group that blends into society in general. There are particular traits that settled people use to identify the Traveller apart from the rest of society. A report into Traveller accommodation by Crosscare states:

> "The findings indicate that settled people have a lot of exposure to Travelling People, through seeing them in public places, through reports or accounts of them in the media and through direct, though usually fleeting contacts."[5]

Though settled people have a lot of exposure to Travellers, this is most often from a distance, through second-hand reports, and fleeting interaction. Exposure does not translate into substantive cross-cultural knowledge and learning. Young identifies social groups as being oppressed when one or more of the following conditions are met:

> "(1) the benefits of their work or energy go to others without those others reciprocally benefiting them (exploitation);
> (2) they are excluded from participation in major social activities, which in our society means primarily a workplace (marginalization);
> (3) they live and work under the authority of others, and have little work autonomy and authority over others themselves (powerlessness);
> (4) as a group they are stereotyped at the same time that their experience and situation is invisible in the society in general, and they have little opportunity and little audience for the expression of their experience and perspective on social events (cultural imperialism);
> (5) group members suffer random violence and harassment motivated by group hatred or fear."[6]

Taking these criteria as determining oppression, Travellers fall under at least four of these considerations, especially when they enter into sedentary living. Travellers do not generally form part of Irish social structures, outside of their own group. When sedentarised, Travellers find it much more difficult to maintain independent business ventures, as traditional Traveller business is dependent on nomadism. Traveller members are often subject to harassment or discrimination based on their membership of the Travelling community, even when settled. However, it is point four where there is a clear association with attitudes towards Travellers in Ireland. Members of this group are repeatedly stereotyped, often as thieves and beggars. They have been throughout the history of the Irish State. Una Crowley identifies a time-line of official discourse where Travellers have been identified as 'abject', 'unpatriotic', 'inferior' and 'anti-citizens' as a discourse of exclusion, while attempts were made at sedentarisation and assimilation.[7]

This official discourse also permeates into the general population, where the *otherness* of Travellers is vocalized in the media, and accompanied by statements of politicians. For this volume it is possible only to capture a snapshot of the discourses that are played out in the media, and among politicians.

> Sunday Independent, 28th January 2008. Traveller culture 'is a life of appetite ungoverned by intellect, it is a life worse than the life of beasts…The Tinker culture is without achievement, discipline, reason or intellectual ambition.'
>
> Irish Times, 2nd March 1999 reported that a Mayo Politician stated '[Traveller men] are able bodied men who should be made go out and do FAS courses like everybody else but instead are lying in the sun like pedigree dogs'.
>
> Irish Times, 13th March 1991 'They are dirty and unclean. Travelling people have no respect for themselves and their children". (County Councillor quoted)
>
> Cork Examiner, 13th June 1990 'These people have been a constant headache for towns and cities throughout the country". (County Councillor quoted)
>
> Sunday Independent, 14th April 1996 'The sooner the shotguns are at the ready and these travelling people are put out of our county the better. They are not our people, they aren't natives' (County Councillor at a Waterford County Council meeting).

The media and politicians both reflect and influence the attitudes of society to Travellers. Rather than dealing with objective discussion, discourses tend to generalise and stereotype. Membership of the Travelling community is continually highlighted when a Traveller commits a crime. This is highlighted by one member of the Travelling community in Dublin.

> "We have had a number of scandals in the last 8-10 years in this country, we have heard about the politics and corruption; we have heard about the banks, right, guards, we have heard about the clergy. I have heard spokespersons for each of those groups, being on the media over the last 10 years. This doesn't reflect the behaviour of all guards this is just a handful,

a few bad apples, and I accept that. What happened in Donegal is not reflective of all guards, likewise of some politicians who are taking backhanders on re-zoning. I know some politicians are decent hardworking people for their constituents. Likewise among priests, but when their spokesperson came out and said this is a handful, we are trying to deal with it as best we can, it is not representative of all, that's plausible and it's accepted by the general public, but yet when I am on the media, or Winnie is on the media, talking about the bad behaviour of some Travellers, saying this is not representative of the Traveller community, we are laughed at. Laughed at. What does that tell us? So, it's plausible for the other groups to say this is not reflective of our organization or the people who work in our organization, whether priests or bankers or guards. That's plausible, but it's not plausible if a member of the Travelling community comes on the radio and condemns this behaviour and says we hope you won't penalize the whole Traveller community because of the behaviour of one or two individuals. We are laughed at. They think it's a joke."[8]

While the media regularly applies negative attributes to the group identity, the identification as a member of the Travelling community is not reciprocated when there are positive stories in the news, regarding Travellers.

"My son-in-law lived up in Clare, and he was coming back with my daughter from town, and he seen smoke coming out a flat and he broke the door down and went in and saved the mother and the child, she was a foreign woman, literally he found the baby and brought the two of them out. The next day he was named as' X', not a member of the Travelling community."[9]

Travellers lose their individual identity through discourses which stereotype and marginalize members of the group. A recent article reflects a tendency to impart the attributes of individual members of the Travelling community onto the community itself.

Irish Independent 31st March 2009: 'The Traveller way of life is dysfunctional and contrary to society and the law. I have found that, in the majority, Travellers need to decide whether to they want to behave in a manner that makes them hated outcasts, or get with the game. It is called responsibility. It is time we stopped pandering to bad behaviour by this "minority"'

The group's identity and the identity of its members are intrinsically linked to Travelling and, while many choose to settle, others continue to attempt to live a nomadic lifestyle. Labelling a nomadic way of life as dysfunctional takes sedentarised society as the yardstick against which worthiness is measured. Nomadic living is considered as the 'other' that has to be viewed as contrary to 'our' way of life because, by its nature, it competes for the physical space that is controlled by sedentarised society, it competes with sedentarised markets and retains values that are gradually being abandoned by 'progression'. Travelling as a way of life is viewed as outside of the law because it cannot fit within 'our' law, a law oriented toward, and designed to regulate, sedentary living. For members of the group, whether settled or sedentary, attitudes of the majority toward the traditional ways of life of the Traveller marginalize and oppress members of the group. When such marginalization and mis-recognition occur it leads to

> "not just a lack of due respect. It can inflict a grievous wound, saddling its victims with a crippling self-hatred. Due recognition is not just a courtesy we owe people. It is a vital human need."[10]

This is not to say that Travellers are saddled with crippling self-hatred, but that recognition can have such an effect on those that suffer from mis-recognition. The question that this section poses is whether this "grievous wound" and "crippling self-hatred" exist for Travellers as a consequence of the lack of recognition of the validity of its tradition of nomadism. The question is whether this mis-recognition is such that it infringes on the autonomy of the individual to an extent that it forces individuals below the threshold of normative agents. This question of a threshold of normative agency for those affected by mis-recognition of a Travelling way of life is very difficult to answer, again, without significant research into the effects on individual members of the Travelling community. What is clear is that nomadism remains central to the identity of a Traveller, even when that person has ceased Travelling. This central part of the identity is held in low esteem by the settled community such that the group may be considered oppressed. Taylor has shown that recognition of identity is of very great importance to the individual.

Earlier, Honneth's argument that mutual recognition plays a role in forming three distinct practical 'relations-to-self' which are vital in forming and maintaining the autonomy of the individual was outlined. These are self-confidence, self-respect and self-esteem. Anderson points out that

> 'In pluralistic and mobile societies, it is difficult to maintain self-esteem in the face of systematic denigration from outside one's sub-culture'.[11]

It may be contested, but there is strong evidence in the media and in political discourse that the Travelling way of life is suffering from systematic denigration. It is not that the way of life suffers from disdain by individuals, based on personal individual taste, but that there are significant elements of sedentarised society who seek to force Travelling to the periphery of society, and to make this way of life extremely difficult to lead.

Human rights are considered to be protections of our status as normative agents, and as such require protecting a person from losing agency.[12] Agency requires liberty, autonomy and minimum provision in pursuing a conception of a worthwhile life. The agency of members of the Travelling community is conceivably threatened in three ways; through loss of self-confidence, loss of self-respect, and loss of self-esteem. This occurs in the face of denigration outside the Traveller sub-culture, both legally and socially, officially and unofficially.

Self-confidence comes from primary relationships, closely identified with childhood relationships of parental love and friendship, but can be impacted in adult relationships as well. Children, who are bullied or deprived of parental love, tend to lack self-confidence. Though less vulnerable, adults are also susceptible to erosion of self-confidence, though often this is a knock-on effect of a lack of recognition in childhood. Under Honneth's conception, self-respect comes from legal recognition of conceptions of one's life. When recognition of these conceptions is denied, or one is formally excluded from society, self-respect can be damaged and autonomy infringed. Self-esteem is grounded in solidarity and social esteem. When one lacks social esteem, or the way of life of a group is scorned and frowned upon by society, self-esteem is impacted by denigration of one's way of life.

From the perspective of Travellers in Ireland, these three practical relations-to-self are threatened in Irish society. Self-confidence, for children, in the formation of autonomy, is affected in schools and in forming friendships as a Traveller way of life is viewed with disdain, forcing children to hide their identity.

> "Even the impact it's having on younger Travellers, and older Travellers, in their day to day life, young people changing their voice, changing the way they dress or that. I can see it having a completely different impact, do you know what I mean. I can see it changing within younger Travellers, within schools and that. Not being accepted. Being the norm is okay, but

being a Traveller in the school I am hiding my identity and talking like a settled person or saying I live in a settled house, because there is so much discrimination there."[13]

Young Travellers can lack self-confidence in relations with wider society. They are unable to give due recognition to their desires, subsuming them underneath the need to 'fit-in' among their peers. Fitting in is a natural desire of young people. Peer recognition is of vital importance. When the Traveller way of life is viewed with disdain, young Travellers are forced to sacrifice desires to maintain a valued way of life. They cannot display pride in their traditional way of life, a way of life many of them maintain in their homes, but on entering the world of sedentary society, a form of 'double-life' is required. For one young Traveller this is the case.

> "I remember when I was in primary school myself in St. Kevin's and an application form came for a three year scholarship within a college there off Parnell St. I went for it. There were around 4 or 500 young lads. There were only 21 places and I got one of them. But when I went to school there was all settled people in it, middle class. I didn't tell them I was a Traveller but some of them knew I was a Traveller. I was hiding my identity while I was there. It was supposed to be a three year scholarship but I only lasted the one. It wasn't meant to be, d'ya know?"[14]

The conflicting pushes and pulls of these two lives force the young Traveller to reject part of him/herself. It is in this respect that self-confidence is linked to autonomy. An autonomous child feels that he/she has real choices in following a preferred way of life; yet when denigrated by society, a Traveller way of life is denied to them. Psychologically, a child is forced to reject part of his/her identity.

Self-respect is affected by the lack of official recognition afforded to a Traveller way of life. Through official stifling restrictions on Travelling, the Traveller way of life is denigrated. Legislation that favours sedentary living, and considers restrictions on Travelling as a means to promoting a sedentary spatial distribution pathologises Travelling. Official discourse such as in parliamentary debates on the 'Traveller problem' treats Travelling as less valuable than sedentary society. The failure of Local Authorities to provide transient halting sites as required under the 1998 Act officially displays a disregard for Traveller life. When Traveller families in unofficial encampments are provided with accommodation, it is primarily in the form of residential 'bricks and mortar' housing rather than preferred transient sites. The association of Travelling with criminality which has been compounded by the Housing (Miscellaneous Provisions)

Act of 2002 creates an official discourse of Travelling as aberrant. Travellers are viewed as abject, both in political discourse and in the national and local media. All these add-up to creating an official impression that Traveller life is less valuable, less viable and less worthwhile than the lifestyle of modern society. This mis-recognition leads to what Honneth describes as a lack of *self-respect.* When this happens, the autonomy of the Traveller, especially the Traveller who prefers to travel, for whom Travelling is a rational choice, is affected. The official discourse creates a negative attitude toward ones ability to make decisions regarding one's choice of lifestyle. A Traveller no longer has a true choice in deciding what is a worthwhile life. The choice becomes limited to choosing the societally preferred way of life, or a way of life officially denied. Not only is the choice physically restricted, but psychologically the choice is not a balanced one, but one 'loaded' in favour of sedentary living. It becomes not about worthiness, but practicalities of the choice not being truly viable.

It is not clear whether official recognition of nomadic lifestyle would improve the problem of oppression, but it would contribute to reducing the perception of criminality among Travellers. Provision of decent transient sites would help in removing the stigma of Travellers being viewed as dirty, unclean and a social nuisance, all of which contribute to a negative perception of the Traveller way of life. Recognition of Travellers as a minority group, with a legal right to maintain their nomadic tradition would provide an official legitimacy. Official recognition would protect autonomy that is threatened by a lack of self-respect, but would not necessarily provide for maintaining self-esteem of the Traveller community in terms of recognition from general society. Official legitimacy may not lead to societal legitimacy. In response to whether official recognition would filter down into the general public, one respondent states that:

> "[w]e wouldn't see it is a panacea. It would be a help, it wouldn't change things overnight."[15]

Many Travellers, due to mis-recognition and mis-respect, continue to lack self-esteem, which manifests itself in hiding their identity in social circles.

> "What pressure is some of those Travellers under having to hide who they are? What are they feeling inside that to get on in life, to get employment or housing, they have to hide who they are, to say I am not a Traveller."[16]

Self-esteem, understood as valuing oneself under particular role-descriptions and identities, impacts upon Traveller autonomy. Travellers, in order to gain recognition, hide who they are- in order to earn a living they have to deny their identity. Travellers feel that they have to hide who they are, in order to get on in society. Travellers try to hide characteristics and social markers that identify them as Traveller. Autonomy is limited as individual Travellers feel they can no longer carry out activities associated with their culture and traditions. No longer can they undertake identity related activities, which limits the availability of truly alternative worthwhile lives. Travellers may choose no longer feel able to act like their fellow Travellers when in general society. This may manifest itself ain terms of behaviour, choice of trades, and whether they feel they can Travel in the face of societal contempt. Autonomy is limited when these preferences are denied through mis-recognition.

Though not all Travellers feel the need to hide their identity, these relations are intersubjective and individuals can be, and are, affected differently

> "In terms of identity we see how it is managed. I do think it is connected to nomadism. Over the years, in terms of our work, there are three distinct ways in which Travellers manage their identity. First, you have those Travellers, regardless, who maintain their identity and say, to hell with the rest of society, they are proud and have integrity and no matter what's put in front of them, they won't hide or conceal who they are and that's great, fantastic. Then you have other Travellers who need to be strategic about their identity, they need to manage their identity in certain situations. It may not be advantageous or be to their interest to disclose their identity it might be in the school, workplace or in the pub because if you disclose your identity there will be consequences in terms of racism, discrimination, bullying, harassment or even dismissal in an employment situation. There are Travellers there who are strategic and aware of the consequences in terms of... well is it in my interest to discuss who I am if you think about it in that sense. Then you have the other Traveller, who are just downright ashamed of their identity, who will go to great lengths to conceal who they are, I think that's part of the internalized depression that they have been subjected to."[17]

It is not that all Travellers lose autonomy through having to hide their identity. Not all Travellers lack self-respect, self-confidence, or self-esteem, in the face of mis-recognition. For some however, autonomy is affected as mis-recognition forces Travellers to choose a particular reaction to negative perceptions of their way of life. Mis-recognition manifests itself differently in different individuals. Some are more resistant to the effects of mis-recognition than others. It is the fact that the autonomy is threatened by this mis-recognition that brings it into the realm of concern for human rights.

Honneth argues that self-confidence, self-respect and self-esteem are dependent on mutual recognition, and that autonomy is dependant on these in different ways. While human rights are protections of our status as normative agents, autonomy is protected to provide for a threshold level of normative agency. While this threshold remains indeterminate, the level of autonomy requiring protection remains unclear.

This section has attempted to outline that the status of members of the Traveller community as normative agents is threatened by a lack of self-confidence, self-respect and self-esteem which are related to recognition of identity and a way of life. For Travellers, identity is a way of life intimately tied to nomadism. A right to a nomadic lifestyle may be required to protect the autonomy of the individual. There are counter arguments that claim that discrimination is the problem and not the right to a nomadic life. A further dogmatic approach would be to contend that Traveller behaviour is simply aberrant, and caused by Traveller refusal to adapt to and accept the norms of modern society. However, discrimination is connected to recognition, and official recognition leading to self-respect, through the adaptation of societal spatial organisation by the provision of a network of transient halting sites, can be instrumental in societal recognition, connected to self-esteem and self-confidence. Subsuming the requirements of nomadic lifestyles beneath those of sedentary society is counter-productive in achieving recognition for Travellers. The first step is to afford nomadism, through a structured network of transient halting sites, equal standing alongside a sedentarised mode of living. Acknowledging that further empirical evidence is required to determine the links between nomadism, recognition and the effects on autonomy as a requirement of normative agency, there is a compelling argument for the right to a nomadic lifestyle in order to protect one's status as a normative agent.

Summary

Taking a substantive approach to human rights as a protection of the human status as normative agents, nomadism is not a necessary condition for minimum provision. However, as a normative agent is one who is able to conceive of, and pursue, a conception of a worthwhile life, there are convincing arguments for a human right to live a nomadic life if one is to consider human rights as protectors of the dignity of the individual. Normative agency requires liberty and autonomy in conceiving and pursuing one's idea of a way of life. When the liberty to pursue a nomadic lifestyle, a form of living considered by Travellers to be extremely important, is restricted or denied, then the Traveller's normative agency is infringed. What makes the liberty to lead a nomadic life important enough to fall under the protection of human rights is that when this liberty is restricted, the autonomy of the Traveller can be sufficiently impeded. Autonomy requires a rich array of choices, knowledge of these choices and the mental capacity to evaluate and review one's preferences. Human rights protect autonomy, a requirement of normative agency. When the array of available options is restricted, or knowledge of these options is restricted then autonomy is infringed. It is not clear which options are valuable enough to facilitate reaching the threshold of a normative agent. However, when the option of leading a transient life is denied, then the autonomy of Travellers can be affected, for example, due to the onset of depression and a sense of hopelessness. Mutual recognition is important in the development of self-confidence, self-respect and self-esteem. These three practical relations-to-self are necessary in formation and maintenance of autonomy. The lack of recognition afforded to transient lifestyles damages these three aspects for Travellers. When self-esteem, self-respect and self-confidence are damaged, then autonomy is infringed. Autonomy requires the protection of human rights to maintain the human status as a normative agent, and the liberty to pursue a transient lifestyle through the provision of a network of transient sites, is instrumental in protecting autonomy. When Travellers are perceived as being beneath contempt, and existing outside the bounds of society, rather than pointing an accusing finger at the Travelling community as a group, it is necessary to view the actions of the members of the group in context. In order to regulate sedentary society for sedentarised folks, legislation is created to maintain an orderly society. Peripatetic groups by their nature struggle to fit within the bounds of this regulated framework. Transient people are either restricted or perceived as acting outside the bounds of society: sedentary society. This perception is instrumental in creating an impression of Travellers as criminal and deviant. Further, lack of legal recognition leads to societal mis-recognition, oppressing and marginalising the Travelling community.

PART IV:

EQUALITY AND THE RIGHT TO LIVE A NOMADIC LIFE

Chapter Sixteen

Universality and Minority Rights

In the previous chapter I have sought to determine whether there is a right to live a nomadic life. Using the thesis proposed by James Griffin, that human rights are based on the dignity of the human being, dignity being better defined as normative agency- the ability to conceive of and pursue an idea of a worthwhile life- I have explored whether the right to live a nomadic life falls under the protection of human rights. Normative agency is defined in three parts: liberty- having the freedom to pursue a conception of a worthwhile life; autonomy- the ability to conceive of a conception of a worthwhile life; and minimum provision- enough of the basic material necessities in life that ensure one is not merely surviving or scraping by, but that one is in a position to conceive of various alternatives of a worthwhile life. While the actual definition of minimum provision arguably remains subjective, it is possible to attain a level of minimum provision without recourse to defining a right to lead a nomadic lifestyle. While nomadism may be instrumental in attaining minimum provision, it is not necessary.

For nomadic groups, the freedom to pursue a nomadic lifestyle is a right that ought to be afforded under Griffin's conception of human rights. However, one caveat in this conception is that the liberty must be sufficiently important to justify the austere protection of human rights. Griffin does not clarify what would constitute making a conception of worthwhile life sufficiently important, other than the fact that it is a conception of a worthwhile life, under the definition previously outlined. Accepting Griffin's caveat with reservations, what makes the liberty to pursue a nomadic life sufficiently important is the connection with the third element of normative agency, autonomy. Human rights under this rubric are considered necessary to protect the autonomy of the individual- that is, the ability to conceive of a worthwhile life. Griffin postulates that there is a threshold level of normative agency below which human rights should protect us from falling. Though this threshold remains undefined, as does the relationship between the threshold and the three components of normative agency, I hope that I have developed a reasonably strong argument for protecting the liberty to pursue a nomadic lifestyle. This argument is based on the premise that when the liberty of nomadic groups, and in the case of this volume, Irish Travellers and European Traveller groups such as the Roma, is restricted to such an extent that it is practically impossible to lead a nomadic life, then the autonomy of members of these groups can be impacted to a great extent; conceivably to the degree that they fall below this ill-defined threshold of normative agency. Human rights are required to ensure the protection of the human status as normative agents.

The last section focused on the relationship between autonomy, and Axel Honneth's Struggle for Recognition.[1] Honneth proposes, but by no means confirms, that autonomy is related to reciprocated recognition, between individuals and society, but also minority sub-groups and larger society. Recognition, as outlined earlier, is linked to self-esteem, self-confidence and self-respect, each of which is instrumental in preserving autonomy. When the way of life of a group, such as Travellers, is denigrated, rendered unlawful and/or viewed with disdain among society in general, this has a reciprocal effect on members of that group. Self-esteem, self-respect and self-confidence, can be damaged, affecting the autonomy of members of the group. While I have attempted to draw on conversations with members of the Travelling community, and research by Jean-Pierre Liegeois on the Roma community in Europe, there is compelling evidence that the autonomy of members of the group is affected by restrictions on nomadism- whether due to lack of recognition in law, or lack of recognition among greater society.

If we accept the hypothesis that human rights are invoked in the protection of nomadism, the correct course of action would be to protect that right outright. However, nomadism is not a requirement for maintaining the threshold of normative agency for all members of society. As can clearly be seen, members of sedentary society are not falling below the threshold of normative agency though the right to be nomadic is no more freely available to them than it is to Traveller groups. This leads us to a number of conundrums. The first of these is that in human rights discourse, human rights are considered to be universal; rights afforded to every member of the human family. Liberty rights are historically considered to be doubly-universal: rights of everybody, with a correlative duty on everybody to uphold these rights.[2] Nomadism, if only a right for members of groups whose autonomy is impacted when the freedom to be nomadic is restricted, cannot be considered to be universal. Griffin attempts to deal with the issue of universality. Griffin claims that the universality of human rights apply only to the highest level rights: autonomy, liberty and minimum provision.

> "We must keep in mind the distinction between basic rights and applied or derived rights. Rights may be expressed at different levels of abstraction… Freedom of expression is derived from…autonomy and liberty. Freedom of the press is derived in certain social circumstances, from freedom of expression."[3]

It is with this in mind that we must consider that the right to be nomadic is derived in certain social circumstances from autonomy and liberty. Autonomy and liberty remain the universal parameters, though nomadism is particular to groups whose conception of a worthwhile life involves this notion, and the liberty to pursue it.

The question that remains to be answered is; in societies that are generally sedentary, how should the human right to lead a nomadic lifestyle be catered for? Ensuring a general right to be nomadic for all of society, would be granting a human right to groups, or individuals who seek the liberty to pursue a nomadic life, but to whom it may not be sufficiently important- restrictions on their nomadism would not impact on their autonomy. Providing for this abstracted right for society in general may place burdens on a society to provide for groups for whom this right is not sufficiently important to be classified as a human right. Intuition seems to tell us that this does not make sense. How the right to be nomadic can be incorporated into societies that are essentially oriented towards sedentarism is the second conundrum of this volume.[4] However, it is not within the scope of this volume to outline the practical measures that need to be taken to ensure nomadism is facilitated in the Irish State, for Irish Travellers. Without going into detail, it may be noted that according to Dr. Colm Power, the following approach ought to be considered

> "Accommodation for Travellers must be appropriately designed to meet their varied social, extended family and economic needs. Government and Local Aothorities should both provide and facilitate a range of site provision ranging from a national network of traditional and new temporary halting or transit sites, linked to good quality, well located and sensitively planned and managed private and public permanent sites. Accommodation policies should be informed and developed in an integrated way that takes into account the specific health, education, economic, employment and training needs of Travellers and the protection

of Traveller culture. A co-ordinated, holistic approach to these interrelated needs is required to improve services for Irish Travellers taking into account, that for many Travellers, their accommodation space is also their workplace."[5]

There are a number of ways in which minority rights are considered when they are in conflict with the aims of the majority society. Human rights are, practically speaking, one way in which utilitarianism is restricted, to ensure that certain issues, of a particular fundamental importance to the individual, are not subsumed beneath the general will of society. Many states established since the end of the colonialism, in a post-World War II world, have included Bills of Rights in their constitution. South Africa is one such country whose Bill of Rights is viewed as being a solution to, and a medium for overcoming, apartheid toward the end of the twentieth century.[6] The Bill of Rights attempts to ensure the wrong-doings of the past under the apartheid state are not repeated, but also ensured the willing participation of the white minority in the transition to a multi-cultural democratic inclusive state. The forthcoming Northern Ireland Bill of Rights was a cornerstone of the Good Friday Peace Agreement.[7] Constitutions themselves can provide the framework for protection of the individual. However, there are no existing examples whereby the right to be nomadic is protected in constitutions or bills of rights to date. The question remains as to how the right to be nomadic can be incorporated into the Irish situation, as outlined in the beginning of this volume.

In the resolution of conflicts, minority rights are protected in the political framework that is established, through a number of mechanisms. Christine Bell outlines a number of solutions which can be achieved when negotiating for self-determination.

a) Consociational practice: territorial divisions of power
    a. Autonomy and confederal arrangements
    b. Creating a polycommunal federation where internal boundaries closely correspond to ethnic racial lines.
b) Consociational practice: decision rules
    a. Adopting proportional representation and consensus rules in the executive
    b. Adopting a highly proportional electoral system
c) Consociational practices: state-ethnic relations
    a. Acknowledging group rights or corporate federalism (i.e. autonomy over spheres such as language or culture

d) Integrative practices: territorial divisions of power
   a. Creating a mixed or non-communal federal structure (where federal boundaries do not relate to ethnic division)
   b. Establishing a single inclusive unitary state
e) Integrative practices: decision rules
   a. Adopting majoritarian but integrated executive, legislative, and administrative decision making
   b. Adopting a semi-majoritarian or semi-proportional electoral system
   c. Adopting ethnicity blind public bodies.[8]

These formulations have been used in the solution to conflicts, and in addressing the requirements of minority groups, or groups in conflict. The particular choice of system is dependant upon circumstances, interaction and trust between groups, differentials in populations, as well as the influence, and desired outcome, of the 'International Community' in the situation. The formulations above do not present viable possibilities for addressing a right to be nomadic, with Traveller numbers making up less than one per cent of the population, without examining the reasons why these approaches would not work, it is only the last one that bears a realistic chance of being implemented. It is arguable that it is already being implemented, and that the 'ethnicity' blind approach has failed to protect the autonomy of the Irish Traveller. Many of the other approaches, considering the small proportion of the population that are members of the Travelling community, would neither be practical or desirable.

This paradox of non-universal rights is one that raises its head in many discussions of minority rights and multiculturalism. While Kymlicka has attempted to address how to deal with minority rights, he does not address the problem of nomadism. Kymlicka highlights four models of multi-cultural citizenship- minority nationalisms, indigenous peoples, immigrant populations, and metics (long term residents who are excluded from the democratic process). Under the four typologies of minority groups discussed by Kymlicka, nomadic groups are absent.[9] Kymlicka himself agrees that the Roma represent a grey area in his analysis[10] as a minority whose homeland is everywhere and nowhere.[11] Travellers may be viewed as having this problem as the focus of sedentary society is on the existence of permanent abodes, yet nomadism is contrary to this conception, always moving from one abode to another.

For subordinated or oppressed groups, Iris Marion Young proposes 'differentiated citizenship'. A form of differentiated citizenship is required to accompany the electoral politics of the countries they inhabit. Young proposes

> "the following principle: a democratic public, however that is constituted, should provide mechanisms for the effective representation and recognition of the distinct voices and perspectives of those of its constituent groups that are oppressed or disadvantaged within it. Such group representation implies institutional mechanisms and public resources supporting three activities: (1) self-organization of group members so that they gain a sense of collective empowerment and a reflective understanding of their collective experience and interests in the context of the society; (2) voicing a group's analysis of how social policy proposals affect them, and generating policy proposals themselves, in institutionalized contexts where decision makers are obliged to show that they have taken these perspectives into consideration; (3) having veto power regarding specific policies that affect a group directly, for example, reproductive rights for women, or use of reservation lands for Native Americans."[12]

The benefits of an institutionalized differentiated citizenship, for Young, are

> "- it facilitates and encourages the self-organisation of members of the group, and creates a sense of empowerment, and collective understanding of the group.
> - it voices the group's analysis of how social policy proposals affect them, generate policy proposals, and requires decision makers to show how they have taken the considerations of the group on board
> - it gives the group veto power over decisions that affect the group directly."[13]

Young views institutionalization of a differentiated citizenship as positive- it allows for different groups with different circumstances to come together and participate together in public institutions. It is not to compensate for any inferiority, but is a positive assertion of different forms of life.[14] However, in order to be effective, this requires a concerted effort by the existing political groups to overcome the problem of origin- the process has to be established by someone. In order to do this, the political actors will be required to prepare political space and initiate legislation that will allow the Traveller groups to be established, and protected from recriminations. This may be difficult to achieve while policy is influenced by politics and introducing legislation favourable to marginalized groups is possibly a death-knell for the politicians who are proponents of such. For issues regarding the conflict between sedentarisation and nomadism, it is unclear how a right to a veto on decisions that affect both ways of life is entirely practical. It is also unclear how an institutionalisation of a differentiated citizenship can undo the policies of the past, or redress existing legislation.

Returning to the discussion of the universality of human rights, I have mentioned earlier that derivations of human rights and the contents of these rights are circumstantial. The right to freedom of the press derives from a right to free expression, and a right to vote is dependant on being part of some form of democratic society. While the right to minimum provision, liberty and autonomy are doubly universal, the 'second-order' rights that are protections of liberty, autonomy and minimum provision need not necessarily be universal. The problem with rights that are not universal, and may be context-specific, and specific only to certain groups and individuals, can be addressed by creating rights that are only rights for certain groups. This has been attempted in various minority cultures such as the establishment of certain minority language rights in Quebec, or through the mechanisms outlined above. In Ireland, establishing a right to be nomadic may be problematic in that there may be groups and individuals whose autonomy and liberty as normative agents is not threatened by denial of this right and will seek to claim this as a right and demand support and provision for this right. Another approach to dealing with this problem is one of equality.[15] Sedentarism is protected by the state through the protection of private property in the constitution. Does equality require that nomadism is equally protected?

CHAPTER SEVENTEEN

EQUALITY AND NOMADISM

In Ireland, the Equal Status Act, mentioned previously, may provide for the rights of members of nomadic groups to be protected. Article 40.1 of the Irish Constitution states:

"All citizens shall, as human persons, be held equal before the law."

For Irish Travellers, the Equal Status Act has been instrumental in protecting Travellers from discrimination of individuals that may occur as a result of their membership of the Traveller community. It has not, to date, been used to protect a right to lead a nomadic lifestyle. This is due to the Irish Courts interpretation of Equality in the Irish Constitution. What is required for the right to be nomadic to be considered under the Equal Status Act is an interpretation of equality that has not been incorporated by the Irish courts to date.

This section will focus on equality in Ireland and how a right to be nomadic can be incorporated under Irish legislation. The section will attempt to show how equality can be viewed substantively rather than facially neutral such that legislation that adversely affects one group more than another may be deemed unconstitutional. In order to do this, I will briefly outline three different conceptions of equality, as proposed by Oran Doyle. Depending on which conception of equality one considers, this influences how the constitutional enshrinement of equality is interpreted in the courts and in evaluating the constitutionality of legislation.

Facially Neutral Conception of Equality

A facially neutral conception of equality is one that provides that a law that treats everyone equally is not discriminatory on the basis of the law itself. In 1977, in *Dooley v Attorney General,* a challenge to the Prohibition of Forcible Entry and Occupation Act 1971[1] claimed that the law discriminated in favour of landowners.[2] However, the courts found that the law made a distinction on the basis of what a person does, rather than who the person is. Under the view taken by the courts, the Housing (Miscellaneous Provisions) Act 2002 would be considered as not being unconstitutional as the law affects everyone equally based on their particular actions, and does not single out any particular group for discriminatory treatment.

This interpretation can be viewed as relevant to the Housing (Miscellaneous Provisions) Act 2002, in another way. It makes a distinction based on what Travellers do –Travelling- as opposed to who they are. However, as has been shown, nomadism forms part of who a Traveller is, and is not simply something they do. It is not so straightforward to make the distinction in the case of people whose identity is wrapped up in, and indeed defined by, what they do- in this case Travelling. Doyle highlights this distinction

> "The measure, though neutral on its face, effects a discrimination between Travellers and non-Travellers in that Travellers will be penalized for pursuing their way of life, while non-Travellers will not be."[3]

A facially neutral view of the law fails to recognize that laws affect distinct groups of people who do not fit in with the majoritarian view of society in a manner different to how they affect the majority of society.

A Process Conception of Equality

A stronger process conception of equality takes a different view of legislation. It looks at the reasons why legislation is enacted. This conception of equality would examine legislation to see if the reasons for the legislation being enacted are discriminatory- referred to as a discriminatory purpose test in United States law. This conception would examine legislation or legislators, to determine whether they are targeting a particular group in society. In the build-up to passing the 2002 Act, the Irish Parliamentary debates discussed the 'problem' of Travellers' encampments, particularly in the Dodder, Rathfarnham. In a number of Parliamentary Debates in the lead up to, and in pushing through, the 2002 Act the problem of Traveller encampments in the Dodder was highlighted

> 5th February 2002, Minister of State at the Department of the Environment and Local Government (Mr. Molloy): "The issue of encroachment on public and private lands by Travellers has been an issue of much genuine

concern recently, particularly in those areas where large scale encampments were involved."[4]

27th March 2002, Minister of State at the Department of the Environment and Local Government (Mr. D. Wallace): "Deputy Gilmore questioned the need for additional legislation given that we already have legislation on this matter. This is not the case and the fact that certain legislation is not enforced is not the root of the problem. If there was legislation to deal with the circumstances on the River Dodder and the many other circumstances which have arisen, it would have been used. This legislation is necessary."[5]

The legislation was enacted with a view to solving a problem which was not necessarily illegal but was considered to be a social nuisance, caused particularly by Travellers. A discriminatory purpose test under a strong process conception of equality may find the legislation unconstitutional as it is directed at a particular group in society. However, a problem with this approach would be that it would encourage those seeking to introduce discriminatory legislation to avoid discussing the reasons for the legislation, and to talk around the issues in order to see the legislation introduced.

Another process conception of equality which can be considered is known a disparate impact approach. A disparate impact approach evaluates legislation by considering whether the proposed legislation impacts on one group more heavily than another. This process conception requires strong justificatory reasons for the introduction of laws that impact on one group of society more heavily than another. One justification for the enactment of the 2002 Act could be the constitutional protection of private property.

For the 2002 Act to be deemed unconstitutional, the Courts would have to adopt this stronger process conception of equality than is currently in use. This process would involve examining legislation from a number of viewpoints-
a) It would have to look beyond direct discrimination, and focus upon indirect discrimination. Two forms of this are disparate impact, and a discriminatory purpose to the legislation.
b) The court would have to examine whether there was compelling reason as to whether the law is necessary.
c) The courts would have to determine whether the legislation achieved its aim.

d) The courts would then have to determine whether the legislation was a good fit between the aim and the means.
e) The requirement of introducing the law would have to be sufficiently strong to justify the disparate impact on a group in society or the discriminatory purpose.

This approach would consider the impact upon the affected group(s) but this consideration would still remain subordinate to the aim of the law. Thus the right to be nomadic could still be subsumed beneath the compelling reasons for introduction of the law

For the Housing (Miscellaneous Provisions) Act 2002, both a discriminatory purpose and a disparate impact on Travellers are clearly identified. It is not clear that there was a compelling reason to introduce the law- the 'problem' of large scale encampments. Despite the media focus and the resistance of local communities, as well as the hygiene and sanitation issues that were perceived, the compulsion for the law is subjective. It is not clear that the legislation would achieve, or has achieved, its aim. Since the enacting of the legislation, it has been used primarily against small-scale encampments and individual Traveller families, rather than in 'solving the problem' of large scale encampments.[6] It is not clear that the legislation is the 'best fit' between the aims of the legislation, and means of achieving them. The problem, if perceived as one of litter and sprawling encampments on unsuitable grounds, rather than the encampments themselves, may have been solved by the provision of suitable services and amenities. The problem, if viewed as a problem of local hostility, may have been solved by ensuring local authorities provided the requisite number of transient sites under the 1998 Act, thus avoiding the extremely large, unplanned encampments. Finally, the question remains as to whether the requirement of dealing with problem of large scale encampments sufficiently urgent to require effectively eliminating the way of life of Traveller?

However, when all is said and done, under a strong process conception of equality, if the aims, means and fit are all fulfilled, then the way of life of the Traveller can still be subordinated to the necessities of society in general. This strong process conception of equality would continue to fail to protect the right to be nomadic, as established earlier in this volume, if the aims, the means and the 'fit' were considered to be sufficiently urgent to justify the proposed restrictions on Travellers.

A Substantive Conception of Equality

The previous conceptions of equality place primacy on the motivation of the actor, in this case the legislator, rather than on the impact of the legislation. What is important under a process conception is the state of mind of the perpetrator of inequality, rather than the effect on the victim of inequality.[7] A process conception of equality is unable to take into account underlying causes of inequality, such as group dynamics, especially those that contribute to a continual inequality between groups in society. Doyle states that 'deep-seated patterns of discrimination are not cognizable to the law.'[8] Formal equality, each person being 'equal before the law', is an example of this. This weak process conception of equality, fails to take into account the inequality that is actually perpetrated by particular laws. Taxation laws that may be facially neutral, but can be designed to favour wealth increase for those already in the higher earning bracket, while subordinating and perpetuating the poverty cycle for the unemployed would be considered unconstitutional. The one-child policy in China may not be directly discriminatory against females but it has inadvertently led to female foeticide and infanticide due to the effect of the legislation, and the preference for a family to have a male child. A substantive conception of equality involves looking at the impact of legislation on particular groups to determine whether legislation impacts disparately on a particular group in a manner that affects some significantly important and valuable aspect of that group, or subjects the group to subordination to the aims of another/majority group. Or, as Doyle states:

> "Whereas a process conception prohibits irrational differentiation, the substantive conception prohibits unjust subordination."[9]

For a substantive conception the view of equality is altered. No longer is the emphasis on the perpetrator, but on the perpetrated. A substantive conception of equality would examine the subordination of women and seek to ensure facially-neutral legislation, for example, around taxation, does not compound the subordination. Subordination of Travellers requires a different analysis. Subordination of Travellers, it is argued, is based on a view that their way of life (nomadism) is inferior to that of sedentary living. Legislation that compounds this subordination in order to facilitate sedentary living would not be considered acceptable under a substantive conception of equality. The autonomy of members of the subordinated group would be considered as a significantly important aspect of the group, as autonomy, forms the basis of normative agency.

When autonomy of members of one group is attacked by legislation, then a substantive approach to equality ought to protect that autonomy

While formal equality is relatively straight forward for judges to apply, a process conception is viewed as manageable, but a substantive conception is argued to require judges to adopt a role unsuited to their capabilities. Judges would have act as sociologists, and possibly psychologists, to determine whether a group is subordinated, and then to determine if legislation further adds to the subordination. In the case of Travellers, it is clear that Travellers are a subordinate group in society. Travellers are identified as a social group, both internally and externally. This group has lower life expectancy, literacy rates, income, and school completion rates than the rest of society. Travellers have higher rates of unemployment. Whatever the opinions of individuals regarding the reasons for these differentials, the fact remains that the Travelling community is a subordinate group in society. A judge should not have any difficulty determining that the Traveller group is subordinate. However, it remains difficult to determine whether a particular legislation, when facially neutral, will continue to subordinate a particular group. That the Housing (Miscellaneous Provisions) Act 2002 can be argued to have a discriminatory effect, based on the discussions in the Oireachtas, it is possible for proponents of the legislation to claim that the Act would not subordinate the group further- perhaps by claiming it will solve the problem of large scale encampments, unsanitary conditions etc. This type of argument need not be addressed here. However, the Housing (Miscellaneous Provisions) Act 2002 is legislation that restricts, and, as outlined in the earlier section on Irish legislation, virtually renders a nomadic lifestyle impossible. This is particularly true when the Act is viewed alongside existing legislation, and the failure of Local Authorities to provide for transient accommodation. The impact of restricting and preventing nomadism on the autonomy of the Traveller has been outlined throughout this volume. Restrictions on Travelling limit the autonomy of the Traveller. Legislation that criminalizes Travelling, portraying Travelling as aberrant and deviant, impacts on the autonomy of the Traveller. In the face of a lack of recognition of the value of a way of life that is intrinsically important, and inherently linked, to the identity of the Traveller, autonomy is restricted. Legislation is making the Travellers' way of life is illegal, and seems to be saying that it is not worthy of legislative protection vis-à-vis sedentary life and the protection of private property. In this manner, the Traveller and Travellers are further subordinated by the 2002 Act. While it is suggested that making these judgments is beyond the capabilities, or the role, of judges, there are other areas where judges are required to make substantive determinations. Successive and progressive judgments determining what constitutes torture shows that judges are capable of making, and required to make, judgments that determine the content of a law, or in this case, the European Convention for the Protection of Human Rights and Fundamental Freedoms. Judges are required to understand and make judgments on complex issues in fields as diverse as the medical and financial professions, issues of ethics and business law.

A substantive conception of equality that is adopted to consider the impact of legislation on each individual, and on individual members of status groups, in society has the potential for ensuring and achieving equality through the law. If existing and proposed legislation is examined in a manner that considers human rights of the individual members of each group, legislation that impacts on the normative agency/autonomy under the conception of human rights proposed in this volume, would preclude the imposition of such laws. Erosion of normative agency/autonomy is not the only factor which can lead to subordination, but it is a very significant factor. Members of subordinated groups, who suffer from a lack of self-respect, self-confidence and self-esteem, in the manner Honneth describes, lose autonomy, and are further subordinated by mis-recognition. If human rights are considered to be the protectors of individuals from utilitarian law that can impact the autonomy/normative agency of certain individuals for the benefit of society or to further a majoritarian viewpoint, a substantive conception of equality, which understands autonomy as a key component of subordination, will ensure that legislation that threatens the human rights of members of minority groups in society, would be deemed unconstitutional. A substantive conception of equality that considered autonomy/normative agency, as one reference for subordination, could be considered. Any legislation that is deemed to impact on autonomy/normative agency of members of particular status groups would be deemed unconstitutional.

Incorporating a substantive conception of equality in Irish Law has not yet occurred. According to Doyle, the cases interpreting Article 40.1 of the Irish Constitution have foreclosed a substantive conception of equality as an interpretation of the equality guarantee.[10] However, this does not mean that this approach should not be addressed. Future case-law may develop an interpretation of the equality guarantee that opens the door to a substantive approach.

An acknowledgement that the freedom to maintain a nomadic existence is a human right of Travellers is sufficient justification for requiring legislation that subordinates this group to the demands of sedentary society to be considered unconstitutional under a substantive conception of equality. A substantive conception of equality would ensure that legislation that subordinates this group and restricts the right to be nomadic would have to be reviewed and changed. The 2002 Act falls under such a category. A substantive conception of equality that protects Travellers from further subordination would protect Travellers from having the right to be nomadic curtailed.

Chapter Eighteen

Substantive Equality and Nomadism in Legislation

The previous section has outlined the different approaches to equality which could be incorporated into Irish legislation. A facially-neutral conception of equality would fail to protect the right of Travellers to live a nomadic life as this conception only looks at formal equality of each individual under the law itself. A law that punishes an individual for what they do, not who they are would be acceptable. For Travellers, the 2002 criminalises them based on their act of trespass, not for who they are. However this conception fails to consider that Travelling is not just what a Traveller does, but is part of who a Traveller is. A process conception would still allow the negative impacts on the autonomy of the Traveller to be subsumed beneath the requirements of society, if the aim of the law is considered sufficiently important to society, the means (stopping Travellers Travelling) appropriate to the aim and of sufficiently good fit. A substantive view of equality however places the impact on members of the subordinate group as the arbiter of equality legislation.

This final section will discuss what a substantive approach to equality would require of legislation and polity in Ireland with respect to the subordination of Travellers? If subordination is considered to be a matter of autonomy/normative agency, then legislation that impacts on the autonomy of the members of the group would come into question. As discussed earlier, legal restriction on nomadism impacts the autonomy of the Traveller, but not members of sedentary society. As a minimum, a substantive account of equality would require legislation that provides for a liberty right to live a transient life. This liberty right may give legal recognition to Travelling as a way of life, affecting the self-respect of members of the group, by validating, rather than vilifying, a chosen way of life. However, the societal perception of nomadism also impacts on the self-esteem of the minority group. Legislating for a way of life can be instrumental in giving that way of life societal legitimacy. However, it may be neither sufficient, nor necessary. It may not be necessary, as society may give positive recognition to nomadism as a way of life progressively through popular discourse; however to date, this has not happened. It has tended to be the opposite- once Travellers learned to seek their rights they became a group to be feared.

> "We were okay when we were quiet and passive and submissive, but now that we are reasonably educated and articulate, have a vocabulary and can participate with policy makers and go on the media and giver our viewpoints there is a backlash. There is a school of thought out there that while it is one thing to have a Traveller who is uneducated being despised, but who is even more despised is the educated Traveller."[1]

It may also be insufficient, as a liberty right will not provide the space in a sedentarised society for Travelling. Without the physical space, Travelling will continue to be viewed as existing outside of general society. Many of the same practical problems will continue to persist- overcrowding, large scale encampments, unsanitary conditions, etc. A group that is pushed to the margins of society struggles to access services. A dialogical process of legal recognition and social acceptance is required to be set in motion and a substantive interpretation of equality would be instrumental in this regard. A substantive conception of equality would ensure the constitution protection of equality would over-rule the exigencies of local politics to solve the Traveller 'problem'.

In terms of practicalities, in a society oriented toward sedentary living, a liberty right fails to provide the physical space for a transient lifestyle. For this liberty right to be achieved in practice, our current assumptions regarding spatial fixity would need to be altered. Positive legislation regarding planning and zoning would also have to be adapted to suit the needs of members of transient groups, in a manner that is balanced with the rights and requirements of sedentary population. Legislators would be required to consider a transient lifestyle as a valid way of life. Policy makers would have to include for transient lifestyles in policy and planning. Local authorities would have to be required to, not simply allowed to, provide transient accommodation, in a manner that allows for real and effective Travelling- travelling that allows a Traveller to feel he/she is Travelling consistent with the sense of Travelling as is part of the Travellers identity. Legislators and policy makers would have to consider provisions and services to transient dwellings in the same way that they are considered for sedentary society. This provides a possible outline of the content of the right to be nomadic. However, it is not for an academic to sit down alone and determine what the right entails. A right to be nomadic, based on normative agency/autonomy, grounded in recognition, self-respect, self-confidence and, self-esteem, supposes that sociologists, psychologists, and anthropologists may be of assistance; however I do not believe that this is the case. These professions may be of use in confirming the existence of the right based on the conception of human rights I have outlined, but now that the right is identified, engaging the transient communities in detailing the content of right is the only solution.

A substantive approach to equality in Irish Law would not require that each and every Traveller can roam free, merely that the right to transience is balanced with, not subordinated to, the right to private property as viewed through the lens of sedentarism. However, for sedentary society to understand how this balance is to be achieved cannot be done without understanding the requirements of a transient lifestyle. Those who understand the needs of a transient lifestyle are those that lead, and desire to lead, a nomadic life. Provisions for a transient lifestyle need to be addressed in an inclusive and participatory manner. Majority views tend to be represented through the democratic process, and in a competitive, pluralistic democracy, elected representatives rely on considering the views of society in general in formulating the shape of society. Contestatory democracy creates a forum for policy to be debated and decisions to be justified to those they affect or who disagree with them. Strong democracy encourages engagement with society on a number of levels. However, for subordinated groups, maligned groups even, who sit outside mainstream society, engagement has shown to be ineffective in resisting legislation such as the Housing (Miscellaneous Provisions) Act 2002. The Housing (Traveller Accommodation) Act 1998 gave Local Authorities the right to provide for Traveller accommodation, but not the responsibility or obligation to do so. At the same time the buck was passed from the National Executive to a Local Executive. And all politics, as they say, is local. Without a *prima facie* responsibility to provide for Traveller accommodation - in a manner consistent with the needs of Traveller families[2] - Local Authorities were given license to respond to the dynamics of local politics, and the pressure groups of local residents who object to Travellers Accommodation in their area.

It is for these reasons a constitutional guarantee of equality needs to protect already subordinated groups from further subordination. Subordinated groups, as is the nature of subordination, tend to have much more difficulty accessing the corridors of power. Minority groups, through their lack of numbers, have difficulty accessing the corridors of democracy. Dispersed groups have difficulty speaking with a cohesive voice. Travellers, in Ireland, are a subordinated, dispersed minority. Civic engagement has not proved fruitful in protecting the group from further legislation which discriminates against the group on the basis of what they do- travelling- which is also who they are.

While civic engagement seems to fail, a procedural approach to politics is not the solution either. A procedural approach in politics fails to take into consideration the social aspects of society and their interactions. A procedural liberal approach is predicated on the notion that

> "Each person possesses an inviolability founded on justice that even the welfare of society as a whole cannot override…The rights secured by justice are not subject to the political bargaining or to the calculation of social interests."[3]

Yet the inviolability of one person exists in association with the inviolability of each and every other person. Human rights discourse must account for competing spaces in society, whether between individuals, or in groups. The determination of the content of a right cannot be prescribed in isolation. From a Kantian perspective, the liberal state does not discriminate; the state ought not to assume that one particular way of life is intrinsically more worthwhile than another.[4] When nomadism and sedantarism come into conflict, in a society where the two conceptions of a worthwhile life are competing for the same space, a neutral stance by the state does not provide a solution. A solution can only be found through engagement. Engagement requires that the minority group is truly engaged in 'negotiation' over the distribution and management of space. This brings us back to the old communitarian versus liberalism argument. Procedural liberalism determines contents of the 'right' only as these concepts develop, and the content of the 'right' only becomes clear through contestatory engagement. While the 'Western' world has assumed certain procedural rights that states are bound to uphold, these procedural rights came into existence after witnessing the horrors of war, through contesting and debating the moral wrongness of slavery, through developing and expanding a conception of torture, and through struggle. The rights secured by justice, are only secured once they are recognised as rights, and their content determined. In the sedentary world, a right to be nomadic, and its content, has not yet been secured by our current conception of justice. The contest between sedentarism and nomadism has yet to be resolved. The contest has yet to be truly engaged. Power and control is never given up easily, and the contest between these two ways of life has not been given the space to develop. A theoretical and philosophical struggle will lend support to the engagement of nomadic groups as the content of a right to be nomadic is clarified, yet this requires a commitment of academics and social activists to give attention to the struggle. This has not yet occurred, possibly because it is not viewed as one of the more pressing issues of the day, or possibly because there is an implicit presumption that sedentarism is the more worthwhile world view? Perhaps awareness of the underlying conflict that exists is missing? The struggle will not reach a suitable solution without the involvement and engagement of members of the Travelling community in determining the content of the right.

It is unlikely that a solution exists that will prove a panacea for this problem of the conflict between nomadism and sedentarism. The need of one nomadic group is not the need of another. The solution for economic nomads such as the Traveller in Ireland is certainly different to that of the Bedouin nomad in the Negev Desert. Addressing the requirements of the Saami inside the Arctic Circle will need a different solution. The relation between sedentarism and transhumance poses an altogether different problem. The Kuchis remain a marginalised group in the war-torn country of Afghanistan and risk further marginalisation as state-building is imposed on the country. In each respect, it cannot be expected that a solution can be found that respects and balances the rights of the nomadic groups with the majority sedentarised populations without a space for dialogue, and an understanding and appreciation that nomadism is more than a caprice, but a way of life that is intrinsically valuable in maintaining and forming autonomy and normative agency. A substantive understanding of equality, one that recognises and examines equality based on the effect of legislation on the autonomy of subordinated groups, is required to ensure nomadic groups are not further subsumed under the rubric of state-building, modernising, or the exigencies of a sedentary society.

Summary

Having attempted to establish that there is a human right to live a nomadic life for members of the Travelling community in the previous chapter this volume accepts that not everyone has a human right to be nomadic. For members of sedentary society, not providing the freedom to be nomadic does not reduce individuals below the threshold of normative agency. For members of the Travelling community the previous section has attempted to show that when Travelling is restricted, members of the Travelling community conceivably fall below this difficult-to-define threshold. Thus, it seems that this human right is not universal. This chapter has attempted to look at the practical aspect of including a human right for members of the Travelling community in tandem with sedentary living. Many different approaches to minority rights have been attempted, though none have been required to address the right to be nomadic of minority groups. Minority rights are protected under various constitutions and in many Bills of Rights around the world. Approaches to minority rights have been contingent on the circumstances that existed in a particular place at a particular time. An approach that this section considers is one of equality. The current approach to equality in Ireland is oriented toward a weak process conception of equality. A facially neutral approach to equality fails to protect the rights of the Traveller community to be nomadic as legislation that affects each in the same way based on what one does, rather than who one is, is not unconstitutional. Process conceptions, whether a disparate impact or discriminatory purpose test is used, still provide for the possibility that the right to be nomadic can be overruled by the requirements of the common good and the necessity for a particular law in society. A substantive approach to equality, which looks at subordination of groups in society, examines legislation on how the law perpetuates or facilitates subordination of a particular group. Travellers are members of a subordinated group and restriction on the autonomy of the Traveller further subordinates the group. If equality was approached from a substantive conception, then the 2002 Act would be viewed as unconstitutional. If a substantive approach is adopted, then legislation which further subordinates nomadic groups such as the Irish Traveller would be deemed unconstitutional by the Irish Courts. However, in order to determine whether particular legislation subordinates or perpetuates subordination of Traveller groups, and to implement legislation which provides for the human right to be nomadic, requires the engagement of sedentary and nomadic societies. The right to be nomadic must be balanced with rights of sedentary society, not be subsumed beneath the exigencies of sedentary living.

Conclusion

This volume has attempted to outline a normative approach to determining human rights and the content of these rights. Human rights are required to protect the status of the individual as a normative agent. Normative agency is the ability to conceive of and pursue this conception of a worthwhile life. According to Griffin, this requires autonomy, liberty and minimum provision. Liberty involves the freedom to pursue a conception of a worthwhile life, while autonomy is the ability to conceive of a conception of a worthwhile life. Autonomy requires a rich array of choices, knowledge of these choices and the mental capacity to understand and review one's preferences. Autonomy is restricted when the array of choices is limited, when knowledge of this array is denied, or when mental capacity is infringed.

Nomadism is a valuable lifestyle choice for Travellers. When this lifestyle choice is denied it is clear the liberty of the Traveller is impacted. However, the argument persists as to whether this lifestyle choice is important enough to require the protection of human rights. For Travellers nomadism carries a very high value. This importance is reflected in the impact on Travellers when the freedom to pursue this lifestyle choice is restricted and due recognition of nomadism as a viable and valid lifestyle is denied. There is a strong argument that autonomy is infringed when this lifestyle choice is denied or restricted. When recognition, whether socially or legally, is denied to the Travellers' way of life, which is intrinsically linked to nomadism, then self-respect, self-esteem and self-confidence, three determinants of autonomy, are damaged. Though further empirical research may be required to determine the extent to which autonomy is infringed, it is evident that nomadism is extremely important to Travellers as a conception of a worthwhile life.

While society is currently oriented to the demands of sedentary living, supporting a right to live a nomadic lifestyle does not require a complete upheaval of the current social order. In order to facilitate transient lifestyles, a balance between the requirements of sedentarised and transient living is required. This requires a sufficient network of transient sites for the Traveller population and for legislation to provide for the possibility of private and public property to be utilised for both sedentary and transient living in a balanced manner. Planning legislation which restricts the possibility of accessing permission to build transient sites needs to be changed. Nomadism for the Irish Travellers does not require unlimited, random roaming, but an agreed, flexible system which allows for a transient lifestyle, balanced with, but not controlled by, the demands of sedentary society. Vital to this demand is that the requirements of Local Authorities to provide transient sites be met, and that legislation such as the 2002 Housing (Miscellaneous Provisions) Act be repealed at least until an equitable balance between transient and sedentary living is achieved in the distribution of public and private property.

In order for the right of the Travelling community to live a nomadic life to be achieved, it is necessary for sedentary society, which holds the reins of power in the Irish nation-state by virtue of numbers, to engage with the Travelling community in determining what is required to achieve this right, balanced with the demands of sedentary living. The content of the right can only be determined once there is a system in place which ensures that the rights of nomadic groups are to be protected. While various minority rights theories and approaches have been proposed and adopted in recent history none of these deal with the complex interplay between nomadic peoples and sedentary living. One possible method of ensuring the rights which protect the normative agency of nomadic groups in Ireland is through the constitutional guarantee of equality. However, the current approach to equality is not sufficient to ensure that minority groups which are marginalised have their autonomy protected. A substantive approach to equality examines legislation from the perspective of whether the legislation contributes to or perpetuates the subordination of minority groups. The impact of legislation such as the Housing (Miscellaneous Provisions) Act of 2002 on the autonomy/agency of members of the Travelling community would be viewed as unconstitutional under a substantive approach to equality. This legislation would be required to be reviewed and amended to protect the autonomy of members of the Travelling community, which requires the liberty to pursue a nomadic existence.

While individuals cannot and should not be required to personally approve of, or promote, a way of life they may find disagreeable, human rights are required to protect individual members of minority group from having their autonomy infringed by the preferences of the majority. Legal recognition of Travelling as an acceptable way of life is instrumental in protecting the autonomy of Travellers. Legal recognition may not provide the social recognition that is also instrumental in realising autonomy through self-esteem, but it has a very important role to play. The attitudes of society to nomadic groups, and Travellers in Ireland, may be based on the prevailing view that members of these groups are criminal and deviant. Elevated levels of crime, unemployment, alcoholism, anti-social behaviour etc among members of these groups may provide evidence for some that this is indeed true. However, Irish society should not ignore the role that sedentary society has played in bringing about this scenario. Rather than viewing these statistics as being caused by Travelling, or some inherent defect in the minority group, the role of a lack of recognition and continued subordination of Traveller groups should be acknowledged and redressed. The problems encountered by a minority group while living within the confines of a societal framework which is anathema to nomadism should be contextualised. Rather than introducing legislation as a means to solving the 'problem' of Travelling, legislation should treat the autonomy of Travellers as an end in itself. Restrictions on Travelling to the point that Travelling is 'nothing more liberating than moving from one criminal trespass charge to another' clearly affects the normative agency of members of the Travelling community. Liberty is restricted. Autonomy is affected and limited through a lack of recognition, causing a loss of self-respect, self-esteem, and self-confidence among members of the Travelling community. If society is to truly embrace human rights that treat individuals as an end in themselves, then for members of the Travelling community, and for members of most nomadic groups, freedom to pursue a nomadic lifestyle must be protected through legislation. Sedentary society must accept the role that it has played in subordinating nomadic groups and that further subordination through legislation such as the 2002 Act is contrary to our present-day understanding of human rights.

NOTES

Introduction

[1] Book of Genesis, Chapter 4. Verses 2-9

[2] For those unfamiliar with Ireland, the term Irish Traveller, or Traveller, is a proper noun, and refers to a social group who has maintained a transient lifestyle in Ireland for a number of centuries, though the origin of the group remains contested. For a background on the debates of the origin of the Irish Traveller see: Hayes, M. (2006) *Irish Travellers: Representations and Realities* Dublin: Liffey Press

[3] The Equal Status Act (2000) Act of the Oireachtas, No. 8 of 2000, Part 1, §1 states: " 'Traveller community' means the community of people who are commonly called Travellers and who are identified (both by themselves and others) as people with a shared history, culture and traditions including, historically**, a nomadic way of life** on the island of Ireland."(my emphasis)

[4] Gilbert, J. (2007) 'Nomadic Territories: A Human Rights Approach to Nomadic Peoples' Land Rights' *Human Rights Law Review,* 7 (4), p. 684

[5] Niner, P. (2004) 'Accommodating Nomadism? An Examination of Accommodation Options for Gypsies and Travellers in England' *Housing Studies,* 19(2), p. 144

[6] Central Statistics Office- Census 2006, Volume 5, Table 1 Available from: http://www.cso.ie/census/census2006results/volume_5/Tables_1_to_11.pdf

[7] Central Statistics Office- Census 2006, Volume 5, Table 35 A-B Available from: http://www.cso.ie/census/census2006results/volume_5/Tables_34_to_44.pdf

[8] Okely, J. (1983) 'The Traveller Gypsies'. Quoted in: O' Reilly, M. (1993) *With Travellers- A Handbook for Teachers* Dublin: Blackrock Teachers' Centre, p. 10

[9] Commission on Itinerancy (1963) *Report of the Commission on Itinerancy*, Dublin: The Stationery Office, p. 34

[10] Ibid, p. 37

[11] Barany, Z. (2002) 'Ethnic Mobilisation without Pre-requisites: The East European Gypsies' *World Politics*, 54 (3), p. 290

[12] Special Eurobarometer Survey 296, July 2008, Discrimination in the European Union, Experiences and Attitudes, p8

[13] Barany, Z. (2002) 'Ethnic Mobilisation without Pre-requisites: The East European Gypsies' *World Politics*, 54 (3), p. 285

[14] Bancroft, A. (2005) Roma *and Gypsy-Travellers in Europe: Modernity, Race, Space and Exclusion* Hants: Ashgate Publishing, p. 1

[15] Interestingly, though the various dialects may be unintelligible across many 'tribes', it is the common roots of the dialects that have been used to trace the Romany origins to India, to their exodus around the 13th century.

[16] Kovats, M. (2003) 'The Politics of Roma Identity: Between Nationalism and Destitution' p. 2, *Open Democracy* www.opendemocracy.net A Romany non-territorial national identity is increasingly recognized in international fora, such as the Council of Europe and the United Nations. This is an unusual occurrence as national identities are usually very closely associated to a particular territory.

[17] Excerpt from Focus Group Discussion in Pavee Point, 22nd July 2009, Male 22 years old

[18] Excerpt from Focus Group Discussion in Pavee Point, 22nd July 2009, Female, mother of seven children.

[19] Excerpt from Focus Group Discussion in Pavee Point, 22nd July 2009, Male, 43 years old.

[20] Assimilation has been attempted in Ireland in the early years of the Irish State and acknowledging the failure of this, an integrationist approach has been adopted. In Europe, the nomadic Gypsy Travellers were subject to slavery in Wallachia for over 400 years, while during WWII approximately one third of the Gypsy population was killed during the Holocaust.

Chapter One

[1] Gilbert, J. (2007) 'Nomadic Territories: A Human Rights Approach to Nomadic Peoples' Land Rights' *Human Rights Law Review,* 7 (4), p. 688

[2] Locke, J. (1924) *Two Treatise of Government* London: Dent. Quoted in: Gilbert, J. (2007) 'Nomadic Territories: A Human Rights Approach to Nomadic Peoples' Land Rights' *Human Rights Law Review,* 7 (4), p. 685

[3] Nozick, R. (1974), *Anarchy, State and Utopia* Carlton: Blackwell, p. 174

[4] Vattel, E. (1758) *Le Droit Des Gens, ou Principes de la Loi Naturelle,* Quoted in : Gilbert, J. (2007) 'Nomadic Territories: A Human Rights Approach to Nomadic Peoples' Land Rights' *Human Rights Law Review,* 7 (4), p. 7

[5] Lawrence, T.J. (1914) *The Principles of International Law,* London: Macmillan. Quoted in: Gilbert, J. (2007) 'Nomadic Territories: A Human Rights Approach to Nomadic Peoples' Land Rights' *Human Rights Law Review,* 7 (4), p. 687

[6] Western Sahara, Advisory Opinion, ICJ Reports, p.12, para. 152. Available from: http://www.icj-cij.org/docket/files/61/6195.pdf [Accessed 9 June 2009]

[7] ILO Convention No. 169, Article 14. Available from: http://www.unhchr.ch/html/menu3/b/62.htm [Accessed 9 June 2009] The full text of the Article states: 'The rights of ownership and possession of the peoples concerned over the lands which they traditionally occupy shall be recognised. In addition, measures shall be taken in appropriate cases to safeguard the right of the peoples concerned to use lands not exclusively occupied by them, but to which they have traditionally had access for their subsistence and traditional activities. Particular attention shall be paid to the situation of nomadic peoples and shifting cultivators in this respect'. This Convention was only ratified by 20 member states.

[8] Cobo, M., Study of the Problem of Discrimination against Indigenous Populations E/CN.4/Sub.2/1986/7/Add.4. Quoted In: Gilbert, J. (2007), p694. UN Special Rapporteur, Martinez Cobo's definition of Indigenous people is generally accepted as authoritative.

Chapter Two

[1] International Covenant on Civil and Political Rights (1976) Part III, Article 27. Available from http://www.unhchr.ch/html/menu3/b/a_ccpr.htm [Accessed 5 June 2009]

[2] General Comment No. 23: The rights of minorities (Art. 27) (1994) CCPR/C/21/Rev.1/Add.5, para. 5.2 Available from:
http://www.unhchr.ch/tbs/doc.nsf/(Symbol)/fb7fb12c2fb8bb21c12563ed004df111?Opendocument [Accessed 5 June 2009]

[3] UNESCO Universal Declaration on Cultural Diversity, (2001) Preamble. Available from: http://www2.ohchr.org/English/law/diversity.htm [Accessed 5 June 2009]

[4] The Equal Status Act (2000) Act of the Oireachtas, No. 8 of 2000, Part 1, §1

[5] Submission by the Irish State to the Committee for the Elimination of Racial Discrimination CERD/C/460/Add.1, para. 27 Available from:
http://www.unhchr.ch/tbs/doc.nsf/898586b1dc7b4043c1256a450044f331/406b61b6eff7296ec1256f3900300005/$FILE/G0442321.pdf [Accessed 7 June 2009]

[6] General Comment No. 23: The rights of minorities (Art. 27) (1994) CCPR/C/21/Rev.1/Add.5, para. 5.2 Available from:
http://www.unhchr.ch/tbs/doc.nsf/(Symbol)/fb7fb12c2fb8bb21c12563ed004df111?Opendocument [Accessed 5 June 2009]

[7] Ethnicity is debated and what the objective criteria are in defining ethnicity is not further elaborated upon. The process of defining ethnicity has moved from one which centred upon race as a particular separating factor, through debating the social constructivist approach to ethnic definition such as influenced by social entrepreneurs who attempt to 'manufacture' ethnic division such as in the lead up to the Balkan Wars or in Rwanda under Belgian occupation. More recent discourses on ethnicity focus on identification and self-identification and regard ethnicity as fluid concept. The debate between a primordial and a constructivist approach continues.

[8] *Mandla v. Dowell-Lee* [1983] 2 AC 548 House of Lords: The 'Mandla Criteria', drawn up by the House of Lords after the case of Mandla v Lee relating to Sikhs in 1983, on what constitutes an ethnic group.

[9] Bancroft, A., (2005) Roma and Gypsy-Travellers in Europe: Modernity, Race, Space and Exclusion Ashgate Publishing, p. 16. Bancroft highlights one of the consequences, and perhaps aims of denial of ethnicity 'Deconstructing 'ethnicity' can be politically damaging to the ethnic group on the receiving end, especially when their deconstruction is followed by a reconstruction as a socially delinquent subculture'.

[10] Equality Authority (2006) *Traveller Ethnicity* An Equality Authority Report, p. 55 Available from: http://www.equality.ie/getFile.asp?FC_ID=264&docID=556 [Accessed 2 July 2009]

[11] Concluding Observations of the Human Rights Committee on Ireland's Third Periodic Report, 2008 CCPR/C/IRL/CO/3, para. 23. Available from: http://www.universalhumanrightsindex.org/hrsearch/displayDocumentVersions.do;jsessionid=D2B61415A51C6DCE055F77058248E836?lang=en&docId=1436 [Accessed 7 June 2009]

[12] Framework Convention for the Protection of National Minorities, Council of Europe. Available from: http://www.coe.int/t/dghl/monitoring/minorities/1_AtGlance/PDF_H(1995)010_FCNM_ExplanReport_en.pdf [Accessed 7 June 2009]

[13] Report Submitted by Ireland Pursuant to Article 25, Paragraph 1 of the Framework Convention for the Protection of National Minorities, ACFC/SR(2001)006, p. 17 Available from: http://www.coe.int/t/dghl/monitoring/minorities/3_FCNMdocs/PDF_1st_SR_Ireland_en.pdf [Accessed 7 June 2009]

[14] Bunreacht na hEireann, Article 15 §2(1) 'The sole and exclusive power of making laws for the State is hereby vested in the Oireachtas: no other legislative authority has power to make laws for the State'. Bunreacht na hEireann, Article 15 §2(1)

[15] European Convention on Human Rights Act (2003) Act of the Oireachtas, No. 20 of 2003, § 2(1) 'In interpreting and applying any statutory provision or rule of law, a court shall, in so far as is possible, subject to the rules of law relating to such interpretation and application, do so in a manner compatible with the State's obligations under the Convention provisions'.

[16] European Convention on Human Rights Act (2003) Act of the Oireachtas, No. 20 of 2003, § 3(1) 'Subject to any statutory provision (other than this Act) or rule of law, every organ of the State shall perform its functions in a manner compatible with the State's obligations under the Convention provisions.'

[17] European Convention on the Protection of Human Rights and Fundamental Freedoms, Article 8. The full article is as follows: 1. Everyone has the right to respect for his private and family life, his home and his correspondence. 2. There shall be no interference by a public authority with the exercise of this right except such as is in accordance with the law and is necessary in a democratic society in the interests of national security, public safety or the economic well-being of the country, for the prevention of disorder or crime, for the protection of health or morals, or for the protection of the rights and freedoms of others.

[18] *Chapman v. the United Kingdom*, [2001] 27328/95 ECHR, § 96, 2001. The full paragraph reads as follows: Nonetheless, although the fact of belonging to a minority with a traditional lifestyle different from that of the majority does not confer an immunity from general laws intended to safeguard the assets of the community as a whole, such as the environment, it may have an incidence on the manner in which such laws are to be implemented. As intimated in *Buckley*, the vulnerable position of Gypsies as a minority means that some special consideration should be given to their needs and their different lifestyle both in the relevant

regulatory planning framework and in reaching decisions in particular cases (judgment cited above, pp. 1292-95, §§ 76, 80 and 84). To this extent, there is thus a positive obligation imposed on the Contracting States by virtue of Article 8 to facilitate the Gypsy way of life (see, *mutatis mutandis*, *Marckx v. Belgium*, judgment of 13 June 1979, Series A no. 31, p. 15, § 31; *Keegan v. Ireland*, judgment of 26 May 1994, Series A no. 290, p. 19, § 49; and *Kroon and Others v. the Netherlands*, judgment of 27 October 1994, Series A no. 297-C, p. 56, § 31).

[19] The Equal Status Act (2000) Act of the Oireachtas, No. 8 of 2000, Part 1, §1.

Chapter Three

[1] Bunreacht na hEireann, Article 3, § 1

[2] Byrne, R. & Binchy, W. (2002) *Annual Review of Irish Law 2002* Dublin: Thomson Roundhall pp. 538-606

[3] The Housing Miscellaneous Provisions Act (2002) Act of the Oireachtas, No. 9 of 2002

The Equal Status Act (2000) Act of the Oireachtas, No. 8 of 2000, Part 1, §1

The Roads Act (1993) Act of the Oireachtas, No. 14 of 1993

The Housing (Traveller Accommodation) Act (1998) Act of the Oireachtas, No.33 of 1998

[4] Crowley, U. (2007) 'Boundaries of Citizenship: The Continued Exclusion of Travellers'. In: Hayward, K. & MacCarthiagh, H. eds. *Recycling the State: The Politics of Adaptation in Ireland* Irish Academic Press, p. 101

[5] The Housing (Traveller Accommodation) Act (1998) Act of the Oireachtas, No.33 of 1998, § 19-22

[6] Irish Human Rights Commission (2008) *Travellers Cultural Rights: The Right to Respect for Traveller Culture and Way of Life* A Research Report by the Irish Human Rights Commission and Pavee Point Traveller Centre, p. 29

[7] The Housing (Traveller Accommodation) Act (1998) Act of the Oireachtas, No.33 of 1998, Part III, §32

[8] Advisory Committee on the FCNM, Second Opinion on Ireland adopted 6 October 2006, ACFC/OP/II(2006)007, para. 59. Available from:
http://www.coe.int/t/dghl/monitoring/minorities/3_FCNMdocs/PDF_2nd_OP_Ireland_en.pdf [Accessed 10 June 2009]. The Advisory Committee state: ' While noting the persisting delivery shortcomings in terns of permanent housing, the Advisory Committee considers the lack of appropriate transient halting sites continues to be one of the key problems relating to the accommodation of Travellers'.

[9] Irish Traveller Movement (2002) *Charting a Future Strategy for the Delivery of Traveller Accommodation* A Research Report by the Irish Traveller Movement, p. 5 Available from: http://www.itmtrav.ie/publications/Accom-Strategy.html [Accessed 27 May 2009]

[10] Crowley, U. (2007) 'Boundaries of Citizenship: The Continued Exclusion of Travellers'. In: Hayward, K. & MacCarthiagh, H. eds. *Recycling the State: The Politics of Adaptation in Ireland* Irish Academic Press, p. 105

[11] Byrne, R. & Binchy, W. (2002) *Annual Review of Irish Law 2002* Dublin: Thomson Roundhall, p. 538 'Trespass to land is tort' "Trespass, of itself, is not generally a criminal offence... a civil remedy is normally the only legal response to trespass'.

[12] The Housing Miscellaneous Provisions Act (2002) Act of the Oireachtas, No. 9 of 2002, Part 3, Section 24 amending the Criminal Justice (Public Order) Act (1994) Part IIA, §19F

[13] The Housing Miscellaneous Provisions Act (2002) Act of the Oireachtas, No. 9 of 2002, Part 3, Section 24 amending the Criminal Justice (Public Order) Act (1994) Part IIA, §19G(1) 'A person guilty of an offence under this Part shall be liable on summary conviction to a fine not exceeding €3,000 or to a term of imprisonment not exceeding one month or to both'.

[14] Byrne, R. & Binchy, W. (2002) *Annual Review of Irish Law 2002* Dublin: Thomson Roundhall, pp. 578-580

[15] Bunreacht na hEireann, Article 38, §1

[16] Byrne, R. & Binchy, W. (2002) *Annual Review of Irish Law 2002* Dublin: Thomson Roundhall, p. 578

[17] The Housing Miscellaneous Provisions Act (2002) Act of the Oireachtas, No. 9 of 2002, Part 3, Section 24 amending the Criminal Justice (Public Order) Act (1994) Part IIA, §19G(2)

[18] Byrne, R. & Binchy, W. (2002) *Annual Review of Irish Law 2002* Dublin: Thomson Roundhall, p. 551

[19] Bunreacht na hEireann, Article 40 §1

[20] Byrne, R. & Binchy, W. (2002) *Annual Review of Irish Law 2002* Dublin: Thomson Roundhall p. 580

[21] Doyle, O. (2004) *Constitutional Equality Law* Dublin: Thomson Roundhall, p. 237

[22] Norris v. Attorney General [1984] I.R. 36 Quoted in: Doyle, O. (2004) *Constitutional Equality Law* Dublin: Thomson Roundhall, p. 237. McWilliams, J. states 'A certain act is declared to be unlawful. It may be performed by either homosexual or heterosexual men with either men or women. Although it is perfectly obvious that such acts will usually be performed between homosexual males, which is probably what the legislature had in mind that does not constitute an invidious or arbitrary discrimination between homosexuals citizens and more than the statutes making theft an offence constitute an invidious or arbitrary discrimination against congenital kleptomaniacs, supposing there were such a group of people'.

[23] Parliamentary Debates, Dáil Éireann - Volume 547 - 05 February, 2002. Available from: http://www.oireachtas-debates.gov.ie/D/0547/D.0547.200202050019.html [Accessed 11 June 2009]

[24] Byrne, R. & Binchy, W. (2002) *Annual Review of Irish Law 2002* Dublin: Thomson Roundhall, p. 580

[25] Ibid, p. 582

[26] Bunreacht na hEireann, Article 40 §5

[27] DPP. V. Dunne [1994] 2 I.R. 537 Quoted in: Byrne, R. & Binchy, W. (2002) *Annual Review of Irish Law 2002* Dublin: Thomson Roundhall, p. 575
[28] The Housing Miscellaneous Provisions Act (2002) Act of the Oireachtas, No. 9 of 2002, Part 3, Section 24 amending the Criminal Justice (Public Order) Act (1994) Part IIA, §19F.
[29] Casey, L. (2000) *Constitutional Law in Ireland* Dublin: Roundhall Sweet & Maxwell, p.516
[30] King v. Attorney General, [1981] I.R. 233 Quoted in: Byrne, R. & Binchy, W. (2002) *Annual Review of Irish Law 2002* Dublin: Thomson Roundhall, p. 577 n King v Attorney General [1981] I.R. 233, the Supreme Court struck down a provision which allowed a person to be imprisoned for up to 3 months for loitering with intent to commit a criminal offence, and for a conviction to be secured upon the evidence of one credible witness. It was not necessary to prove that the person suspected was guilty of any particular act or acts tending to show his purpose or intent; the provision allowed a conviction if from the circumstances of the case, and from the accused's "known character as proved" to the court, it appeared to the court that his intent was to commit a felony.
[31] Crowley, U. (2007) 'Boundaries of Citizenship: The Continued Exclusion of Travellers'. In: Hayward, K. & MacCarthiagh, H. eds. *Recycling the State: The Politics of Adaptation in Ireland* Irish Academic Press, p. 105

Chapter Four

[1] Kant, I (1991) *Kant's gesammelte Schriften* 6 p. 230 Quoted in: Griffin, J. (2008) *On Human Rights* New York: Oxford University Press, p. 2
[2] Kant, I (1785) *Groundwork on the Metaphysics of Morals* Quoted in: Lindley, R. (1986) *Autonomy* New Jersey: Humanities Press, p. 13
[3] Dworkin, R. (1981) 'Rights as Trumps'. In: Waldron, J. ed. (1995) *Theories of Rights* New York: Oxford University Press, pp. 153-167
[4] Griffin, J. (2008) *On Human Rights* New York: Oxford University Press, p. 21

Chapter Five

[1] Griffin, J. (2008) *On Human Rights* New York: Oxford University Press, pp. 22-27
[2] Ibid, p. 21
[3] Ingram, A. (1994) *A Political Theory of Rights* Oxford: Clarendon Press, p. 2
[4] Ibid, p. 197
[5] Griffin, J. (2008) *On Human Rights* New York: Oxford University Press, p. 18
[6] Ibid, p. 14

Chapter Six

[1] Ibid, p. 33
[2] Wellman, C. (1997) *An Approach to Rights* Netherlands: Kluwer Academic Publishers, p. 17 Wellman admits to having gone through a professional crisis, when it was pointed out to him that his theory involved the possibility that children would not have rights, but he has resolved this personally, through the realization of children's rights, and the complexity of a full rights theory
[3] Griffin, J. (2008) *On Human Rights* New York: Oxford University Press, p. 19
[4] Ibid, p. 32
[5] Ibid, pp. 37-39. Griffin discusses his interpretation of practicalities.

Chapter Seven

[1] Ibid, p. 45
[2] Ibid, p. 46
[3] Ibid
[4] Ibid, p. 47 Minimum provision is considered as welfare to an extent that human rights require access to basic goods- food, health, water such that one can maintain the functions of a normative agent.

Chapter Eight

[1] Dworkin, G. *The Theory and Practice of Autonomy.* Quoted in: Ingram, A. (1994) *A Political Theory of Rights* Oxford: Clarendon Press, p. 99
[2] Ibid, p. 122
[3] Raz, J, 'The Morality of Freedom'. Quoted in: Ingram, A. (1994) *A Political Theory of Rights* Oxford: Clarendon Press, p. 104
[4] Lindley, R. (1986) *Autonomy* New Jersey: Humanities Press, p. 162
[5] Honneth, A. (1995) *The Struggle for Recognition. The Moral Grammer of Social Conflicts* Cambridge: Polity Press, p. xii. Introduction from Translator Joel Anderson.
[6] Ibid, p. 129
[7] Koppinan, A. (2008) *Essays in Philosophical Moral Psychology* Helsinki: Department of Philosophy, p. 134
[8] Ibid
[9] Ibid
[10] Rawls, J. (1980) 'Kantian Constructivism in Moral Theory' *The Journal of Philosophy*, 77(9): p. 543

Chapter Nine

[1] Griffin, J. (2008) *On Human Rights* New York: Oxford University Press, p. 162
[2] Ibid. Unfortunately there is a sense of circularity in his discussion, as normative agency is a function of liberty, and the level of liberty is defined by normative agency. Griffin fails to address this circularity.
[3] Ibid, p. 45 'Anyone who crosses the borderline is equally inside the class of agents...possesses the status to which we apply high value'
[4] Ibid, p. 160
[5] Ibid, p. 171
[6] Ibid, p. 169

Chapter Ten

[1] Ibid, p. 180
[2] Nozick, R. (1974) *Anarchy State and Utopia* Oxford: Blackwell, p. 169
[3] Griffin, J. (2008) *On Human Rights* New York: Oxford University Press, p. 184
[4] Ibid, p. 149

Chapter Eleven

[1] Excerpt from Focus Group Discussion in Pavee Point, 22nd July 2009, Male, 22 years old
[2] Excerpt from Focus Group Discussion in Pavee Point, 22nd July 2009, Male, 22 years old
[3] Excerpt from Focus Group Discussion in Pavee Point, 22nd July 2009, Male, 22 years old
[4] Excerpt from Focus Group Discussion in Pavee Point, 22nd July 2009, Male, 43 years old

Chapter Twelve

[1] Liegeois, J.P. (1994) *Roma, Gypsies, Travellers* Strasbourg: Council of Europe, p27
[2] McCarthy, D. & McCarthy, P. (1998) *Market Economies: Trading in the Traveller Economy* Dublin: Pavee Point Publications, p. 27 'Nomadism, which is central to Traveller identity, is a feature of the Traveller economy which allows Travellers to access a broad range of economic activities, like country-wide markets.'
Dublin Travellers Education and Development Group (1992) *Recycling the Traveller Economy: Income, Jobs & Wealth Creation* Dublin: Pavee Point Publications, p. 8 'Nomadism is a feature of the Traveller economy that allows Travellers to access a broad range of markets so that marginal activities are rendered economically viable.'

[3] Report of the European Committee on Migration (1995) *The Situation of Gypsies (Roma and Sinti) in Europe* Strasbourg: Council of Europe, para. 33

[4] Similar to Griffin, I believe that human rights do not encompass all of morality. Human rights are a subset of morality and also a subset of justice which is a subset of fairness. Rawls argues for justice as fairness, however, he does not believe that these are interchangeable. One conception of fairness may require that everything be equally divided. Rawls requires that 'social and economic inequalities are to be arranged so that they are to be of the greatest benefit to the least-advantaged members of society *(the difference principle)*. This he considers justice, as fairness. Human rights demand that each person has minimum provision, but not that social and economic inequalities be arranged in such a way.

Chapter Thirteen

[1] Donahue, M., McVeigh, R. & Ward, M. (2004) *Misli Crush Misli* A Research Report for the Irish Traveller Movement (Northern Ireland), p. 23

[2] McDonagh, M. (1994) 'Nomadism in Irish Travellers' Identity'. In: McCann, M., O Siochain, S. & Ruane, J. eds. *Irish Travellers: Culture and Ethnicity* Belfast: Institute of Irish Studies, p. 95 Michael McDonagh is a well-known spokesperson and activist on nomadism and the Irish Traveller

[3] Ibid, p. 98

[4] Niner, P. (2004) 'Accommodating Nomadism? "An Examination of Accommodation Options for Gypsies and Travellers in England" ' *Housing Studies,* 19(2), p. 157

[5] Interview, August 10th, Bray Traveller Community Development Group

[6] Bancroft, A., (2005) *Roma and Gypsy-Travellers in Europe: Modernity, Race, Space and Exclusion* Hants: Ashgate Publishing, p. 76

[7] Ibid.

[8] Donahue, M., McVeigh, R. & Ward, M. (2004) *Misli Crush Misli* A Research Report for the Irish Traveller Movement (Northern Ireland), p. 9

[9] Commission on Itinerancy (1963) *Report of the Commission on Itinerancy*, Dublin: The Stationery Office, p. 11

[10] Ibid, p. 111

[11] Donahue, M., McVeigh, R. & Ward, M. (2004) *Misli Crush Misli* A Research Report for the Irish Traveller Movement (Northern Ireland), p. 33

[12] Task Force Report on the Travelling Community (1995) *Report of the Task Force on the Travelling Community* Dublin: Government Publication Office, p. 289

[13] Bancroft, A., (2005) Roma *and Gypsy-Travellers in Europe: Modernity, Race, Space and Exclusion* Hants: Ashgate Publishing, p. 65

[14] Task Force Report on the Travelling Community (1995) *Report of the Task Force on the Travelling Community* Dublin: Government Publication Office, p. 289

[15] Interview, August 10th, Bray Traveller Community Development Group

[16] Morris, R. & Clements, L. (2002) *At What Cost? The Economics of Gypsy and Traveller Encampments* Bristol: Policy Press, p. 7

[17] Liegeois, J.P. (1994) *Roma, Gypsies, Travellers* Strasbourg: Council of Europe, p. 134. Liegeois cites between 400,000 and 500,000 deaths in WWII. Other estimates fall to 200,000 and some as high as 1.5 million. The word *porrajmos* is a Rom word meaning *devouring* for the Holocaust of WWII.
[18] Bancroft, A., (2005) Roma *and Gypsy-Travellers in Europe: Modernity, Race, Space and Exclusion* Hants: Ashgate Publishing, p. 163
[19] Ibid, p. 161
[20] Byrne, R. & Binchy, W. (2002) *Annual Review of Irish Law 2002* Dublin: Thomson Roundhall, p. 580

Chapter Fourteen

[1] Excerpt from Focus Group Discussion in Pavee Point, 22nd July 2009, Male 22 years old
[2] Dworkin, G. *The Theory and Practice of Autonomy.* Quoted in: Ingram, A. (1994) *A Political Theory of Rights* Oxford: Clarendon Press, p. 99
[3] Lindley, R. (1986) *Autonomy* New Jersey: Humanities Press, p. 110
[4] Ibid, p. 108
[5] Liegeois, J.P. (1994) *Roma, Gypsies, Travellers* Strasbourg: Council of Europe, p. 114
[6] Mary Rose Walker has carried out in-depth research into suicide among Traveller communities. The suicide rate among Travellers continues to increase, while the national suicide rate has declined slightly. Walker does not attempt to draw conclusion regarding the effects of sedentarisation or restricted transient lifestyle. However, one conclusion is that suicide rates are highest on unauthorised encampments. Walker, M.R. (2008) *Suicide among the Irish Traveller Community 2000-2006* A Research Report for the Wicklow Traveller Interagency Group, p. 34
[7] Ibid, p. 104 'Paradoxically, it appears that improvements in the quality of their lives and increased integration with the settled population, have coincided with Traveller society reaching its current problem with regard to suicide.'
[8] Bancroft, A., (2005) *Roma and Gypsy-Travellers in Europe: Modernity, Race, Space and Exclusion* Hants: Ashgate Publishing, p. 72
[9] Ibid
[10] Ibid
[11] Interview, August 10th, Bray Traveller Community Development Group

Chapter Fifteen

[1] Young, I.M. (1989) 'Polity and Group Difference: A Critique of the Ideal of Universal Citizenship' *Ethics,* 99(2), pp. 250-274
[2] Ibid, p. 259
[3] Task Force Report on the Travelling Community (1995) *Report of the Task Force on the Travelling Community* Dublin: Government Publication Office, p. 28
[4] O' Reilly, M. (1993) *With Travellers- A Handbook for Teachers* Dublin: Blackrock Teachers' Centre, p. 10

[5] McKeown, K. & McGrath, B. (1996) *A Study of Accommodation for Travelling People in the Greater Dublin Area* Dublin: Crosscare, p. 182
[6] Young, I.M. (1989) 'Polity and Group Difference: A Critique of the Ideal of Universal Citizenship' *Ethics,* 99(2), p. 261
[7] Crowley, U. (2007) 'Boundaries of Citizenship: The Continued Exclusion of Travellers'. In: Hayward, K. & MacCarthiagh, H. eds. *Recycling the State: The Politics of Adaptation in Ireland* Irish Academic Press, pp. 90-93
[8] Excerpt from Focus Group Discussion in Pavee Point, 22nd July 2009, Male 43 years old
[9] Excerpt from Focus Group Discussion in Pavee Point, 22nd July 2009, Mother of 7 children
[10] Taylor, C. 'The Politics of Recognition' In: Heble, A., Pennee, D.P. & Struthers, J.R. eds. (1997) *New Contexts of Canadian Criticisms,* Peterborough: Broadview Press, p. 98
[11] Honneth, A. (1995) *The Struggle for Recognition. The Moral Grammar of Social Conflicts* Cambridge: Polity Press, p. xviii. Introduction from Translator Joel Anderson.
[12] Griffin, J. (2008) *On Human Rights* New York: Oxford University Press, p. 181
[13] Excerpt from Focus Group Discussion in Pavee Point, 22nd July 2009, Male 22 years old
[14] Ibid
[15] Excerpt from Focus Group Discussion in Pavee Point, 22nd July 2009, Male 43 years old
[16] Excerpt from Focus Group Discussion in Pavee Point, 22nd July 2009, Mother of 7 children
[17] Excerpt from Focus Group Discussion in Pavee Point, 22nd July 2009, Male 43 years old.

Chapter Sixteen

[1] Honneth, A. (1995) *The Struggle for Recognition. The Moral Grammar of Social Conflicts* Cambridge: Polity Press
[2] Griffin, J. (2008) *On Human Rights* New York: Oxford University Press, pp. 48-51
[3] Ibid. p. 50
[4] Sedentarism is a term with dual use. Sedentarism in this case refers societies whose land-use is predominantly based on provision for settled populations in long-term fixed residences. Sedentarism is also used to mean an attitude which is represents sedentary living as a worthwhile lifestyle, and either, subtly or overtly, representing nomadic lifestyles as less worthwhile.
[5] Power, C. (2004) *Room to Roam: England's Irish Travellers* A Research Report Funded by the Community Fund, p. 35
[6] Bell, C. (2000) *Peace Agreements and Human Rights* Oxford University Press, p. 132
[7] Ibid, p. 55
[8] Ibid, p. 121

[9] Kymlicka, W. (2005) Ashgate Publishing, 'Models of Multicultural Citizenship: Comparing Asia and the West'. In: Tan, S. ed. *Challenging Citizenship: Group Membership and Cultural Identity in a Global Age* Aldershot: Ashgate Publishing, p. 111

[10] Kymlicka, W. (2001) *Politics in the Vernacular,* Oxford: Oxford University Press, p. 56

[11] Kymlicka, W. (2001) 'Introduction'. In: Kymlicka, W. & Opalski, M. eds. *Can Liberal Pluralism be Exported,* Oxford University Press, p. 74. One model discussed in the introduction is one of transnational nationhood which Kymlicka agrees is difficult and that there are no Western models for this complex process

[12] Young, I.M. (1989) 'Polity and Group Difference: A Critique of the Ideal of Universal Citizenship' *Ethics,* 99(2), p. 261

[13] Young, I.M. (1989) 'Polity and Group Difference: A Critique of the Ideal of Universal Citizenship' *Ethics,* 99(2), p. 262

[14] Young, I.M. (1989) 'Polity and Group Difference: A Critique of the Ideal of Universal Citizenship' *Ethics,* 99(2), p. 273

[15] This section is attributed to three conceptions of equality as discussed by Oran Doyle in: Doyle, O. (2004) *Constitutional Equality Law* Dublin: Thomson Roundhall. This thesis is not suitable for the elaboration of such a broad subject which touches on many aspects of political theory and justice. However, brief outlines of the three concepts and the possibilities of the third concept being used to protect the rights of Travellers to remain nomadic.

Chapter Seventeen

[1] The Prohibition of Forcible Entry and Occupation Act (1971) Act of the Oireachtas, No.25 of 1971

[2] *Dooley v. Attorney General* [1977] I.R. 205

[3] Doyle, O. (2004) *Constitutional Equality Law* Dublin: Thomson Roundhall., p. 237

[4] Parliamentary Debates, Dáil Éireann - Volume 547 - 05 February, 2002. Available from:
http://www.oireachtas-debates.gov.ie/D/0547/D.0547.200202050019.html
[Accessed 09 December 2009]

[5] Parliamentary Debates, Dáil Éireann - Volume 551 - 27 March, 2002, Available from:
http://historical-debates.oireachtas.ie/D/0551/D.0551.200203270010.html
[Accessed 14 December 2009]

[6] Doyle, O. (2004) *Constitutional Equality Law* Dublin: Thomson Roundhall., p. 235

[7] Ibid, p. 262

[8] Ibid, p. 262

[9] Ibid, p. 265

[10] Ibid, p. 269

Chapter Eighteen

[1] Excerpt from Focus Group Discussion in Pavee Point, 22nd July 2009, Male, 43 years old
[2] I refer to the provision of Traveller Accommodation as a need rather than a requirement, demand or obligation. This is based on the findings of earlier chapters that transience is a right that is needed to maintain a threshold level of agency/autonomy for the Travelling community.
[3] Rawls, J. (1971) *A Theory of Justice* Massachusetts: Harvard University Press, pp. 3-4
[4] Sandel, M. (1996) *Democracy's Discontent: America in search of a public philosophy* Cambridge: Harvard University Press, p. 13

BIBLIOGRAPHY

Research Reports

Report of the European Committee on Migration (1995) *The Situation of Gypsies (Roma and Sinti) in Europe* Strasbourg: Council of Europe. Available from: [Accessed 26 June 2009]

Irish Traveller Movement (2002) *Charting a Future Strategy for the Delivery of Traveller Accommodation* A Research Report by the Irish Traveller Movement. Available from: http://www.itmtrav.ie/publications/Accom-Strategy.html [Accessed 27 May 2009]

Diacon, D. et al (2007) *Out in the Open: Providing Accommodation, Promoting Understanding and Recognizing Rights of Gypsies and Travellers* A Research Report for the Building and Social Housing Foundation. Available from: http://www.bshf.org/published-information/publication.cfm?lang=00&thePubID=80DDC533-15C5-F4C0-992FC2D89E3A6D17 [Accessed 09 May 2009]

Donahue, M., McVeigh, R. & Ward, M. (2004) *Misli Crush Misli* A Research Report for the Irish Traveller Movement (Northern Ireland). Available from: http://www.itmtrav.com/publications/reports.html [Accessed 02 June 2009]

Dublin Travellers Education and Development Group (1992) *Recycling the Traveller Economy: Income, Jobs & Wealth Creation* Dublin: Pavee Point Publications

Equality Authority (2006) *Traveller Ethnicity* An Equality Authority Report. Available from: http://www.equality.ie/getFile.asp?FC_ID=264&docID=556 [Accessed 2 July 2009]

Irish Human Rights Commission (2008) *Travellers Cultural Rights: The Right to Respect for Traveller Culture and Way of Life* A Research Report by the Irish Human Rights Commission and Pavee Point Traveller Centre

Irish Traveller Movement (no date) *Report on the Socio-Economic Consequences of the Control of Horses Act 1996 on the Traveller Community* A Research Report by the Irish Traveller Movement. Available from:

http://www.itmtrav.com/publications/reports.html [Accessed 02 June 2009]
Liegeois, J.P. & Gheorghe, N. (1995) *Roma/Gypsies: A European Minority* A Research Report for the Minority Rights Group
McCarthy, D. & McCarthy, P. (1998) *Market Economies: Trading in the Traveller Economy* Dublin: Pavee Point Publications
McKeown, K. & McGrath, B. (1996) *A Study of Accommodation for Travelling People in the Greater Dublin Area* Dublin: Crosscare
Moore, T., Vine, J. & Pattison, B. (2008) *Review of Gypsy and Traveller Accommodation Assessments Conducted in the East Midlands* A Research Report for the Building and Social Housing Foundation. Available from: http://www.bshf.org/publishedinformation/publication.cfm?lang=00&thePubID=AA769D78-15C5-F4C0-9992E8BE3AE849FE [Accessed 16 May 2009]
Power, C. (2004) *Room to Roam: England's Irish Travellers* A Research Report Funded by the Community Fund. Available from: http://www.irishtraveller.org.uk/wp-content/uploads/2007/08/roomtoroam.pdf [Accessed 21 May 2009]
Ringold, D. (2000) *Roma and the Transition in Central and Eastern Europe: Trends and Challenges* Washington: World Bank Publications
Van der Stoel, M. (2000) *Report on the Situation of Roma and Sinti in the OSCE Area* Organization for Security and Co-operation in Europe High Commissioner on National Minorities. Available from: http://www.osce.org/documents/hcnm/2000/03/241_en.pdf [Accessed 30 June 2009]
Walker, M.R. (2008) *Suicide Among the Irish Traveller Community 2000-2006* A Research Report for the Wicklow Traveller Interagency Group. Available from: http://www.nosp.ie/book.pdf [Accessed 2 July 2009]

Journal Articles

Appiah, A. (2000) 'Stereotypes and the Shaping of Identity' *California Law Review*, 88(1):41-53
Baldwin, T. (2009) 'Recognition: Personal and Political' *Politics Philosophy Economics* 8:311-327
Barany, Z. (1994) 'Living on the Edge: The East European Roma in Postcommunist Politics and Societies' in *Slavic Review,* 53(2):321-344
—. (2002) 'Ethnic Mobilisation without Pre-requisites: The East European Gypsies' *World Politics,* 54(3):277-307

Cooke, M. (1997) 'Authenticity and Autonomy: Taylor, Habermas and the Politics of Recognition' *Political Theory*, 25(2):258:288

Crowley, U. & Kitchin, R. (2007) 'Paradoxical Spaces of Traveller Citizenship in Contemporary Ireland' *Irish Geography,* 40 (2):128-145

Fraser, N. (2000) 'Rethinking Recognition' *New Left Review* 3:107:120

Gilbert, J. (2007) 'Nomadic Territories: A Human Rights Approach to Nomadic Peoples' Land Rights' *Human Rights Law Review,* 7 (4):681-716

Gmelch, G. & Gmelch, S. (1974) 'The Itinerant Settlement Movement: Its Policies and Effects on Irish Travellers' *Studies*, 68:1-16

Kovats, M. (2003) 'The Politics of Roma Identity: Between Nationalism and Destitution' p. 2, *Open Democracy* www.opendemocracy.net

Niner, P. (2004) 'Accommodating Nomadism? 'An Examination of Accommodation Options for Gypsies and Travellers in England' *Housing Studies,* 19(2):141-159

Nordberg, C. (2006) 'Beyond Representation: Newspapers and Citizenship Participation in the Case of a Minority Ethnic Group' *Nordicom Review*, 27(2):87-104

Rawls, J. (1980) 'Kantian Constructivism in Moral Theory' *The Journal of Philosophy*, 77(9): 515:572

Toppinen, P. (2005) 'Critical Reflections on Social Justice and Recognition' *Res Publica,* 11:425-434

Young, I.M. (1989) 'Polity and Group Difference: A Critique of the Ideal of Universal Citizenship' *Ethics,* 99(2):250-274

Books

Acton, T. ed. (1997) *Gypsy Politics and Traveller Identity* Hertfortshire: University of Hertfordshire Press

Bancroft, A., (2005) *Roma and Gypsy-Travellers in Europe: Modernity, Race, Space and Exclusion* Hants: Ashgate Publishing

Barany, Z. (2002) *The East European Gypsies* Cambridge: Cambridge University Press

Byrne, R. & Binchy, W. (2002) *Annual Review of Irish Law 2002* Dublin: Thomson Roundhall

Casey, L. (2000) *Constitutional Law in Ireland* Dublin: Roundhall Sweet & Maxwell

Coxhead, J. (2007) *The Last Bastion of Racism: Gypsies, Travellers and Policing* Trentham Books

Crowe, D. & Kolsti, J. eds. (1991) The *Gypsies of Eastern Europe* M.E. Sharpe. Inc.

Doyle, O. (2004) *Constitutional Equality Law* Dublin: Thomson Roundhall
Waldron, J. ed. (1995) *Theories of Rights* New York: Oxford University Press
Fanning, B. ed. (2007) *Immigration and Social Change in the Republic of Ireland* Manchester University Press
Fraser, A. (1992) *The Gypsies* Blackwell Publishing
Griffin, J. (2008) *On Human Rights* New York: Oxford University Press
Hayes, M. (2006) *Irish Travellers: Representations and Realities* Dublin: Liffey Press
Hayward, K. & MacCarthiagh, H. eds. *Recycling the State: The Politics of Adaptation in Ireland* Dublin: Irish Academic Press
Heble, A., Pennee, D.P. &Struthers, J.R. (eds) (1997) *New Contexts of Canadian Criticisms*, Peterborough: Broadview Press
Helleiner, J. (2000) *Irish Travellers: Racism and the Politics of Culture* Canada: University of Toronto Press
Honneth, A. (1995) *The Struggle for Recognition. The Moral Grammar of Social Conflicts* Cambridge: Polity Press
Ingram, A. (1994) *A Political Theory of Rights* Oxford: Clarendon Press
Joyce, N. (1985) *Traveller* Dublin: Gill and Macmillan
Kauppinan, A. (2008) *Essays in Philosophical Moral Psychology* Helsinki: Department of Philosophy
Lindley, R. (1986) *Autonomy* New Jersey: Humanities Press
Liegeois, J.P. (1994) *Roma, Gypsies, Travellers* Strasbourg: Council of Europe
Miller, D. ed. (1991) *Liberty* Oxford: Oxford University Press
Morris, R. & Clements, L. (2002) *At What Cost? The Economics of Gypsy and Traveller Encampments* Bristol: Policy Press
McCann, M., Ó Síocháin, S. & Ruane, J. eds. (1994) *Irish Travellers: Culture and Ethnicity* Belfast: Institute of Irish Studies
Nordberg, C. (2007) *Boundaries of Citizenship: The Case of the Roma and the Finnish Nation State* Helsinki: Helsinki University Press
O' Reilly, M. (1993) *With Travellers- A Handbook for Teachers* Dublin: Blackrock Teachers' Centre
Nozick, R. (1974), *Anarchy, State and Utopia* Oxford: Blackwell
Sheehan, E. ed. (2000) *Travellers: Citizens of Ireland* Dublin: Parish of the Travelling People
Waldron, J. ed. (1995) *Theories of Rights* New York: Oxford University Press

Treaty, Covenants and International Agreements

Advisory Committee on the FCNM, Second Opinion on Ireland adopted 6 October 2006, ACFC/OP/II(2006)007. Available from: http://www.coe.int/t/dghl/monitoring/minorities/3_FCNMdocs/PDF_2nd_OP_Ireland_en.pdf [Accessed 10 June 2009].

Cobo, M., Study of the Problem of Discrimination against Indigenous Populations E/CN.4/Sub.2/1986/7/Add.4. Available from: http://www.un.org/esa/socdev/unpfii/en/spdaip.html [Accessed 12 June 2009]

Committee for the Elimination of Racial Discrimination, General Recommendation No. 08: Identification with a particular racial or ethnic group. (1990) Available from: http://www.unhchr.ch/tbs/doc.nsf/(Symbol)/3ae0a87b5bd69d28c12563ee0049800f?Opendocument [Accessed 7 June 2009]

Concluding Observations of the Human Rights Committee on Ireland's Third Periodic Report, 2008 CCPR/C/IRL/CO/3, para. 23. Available from: http://www.universalhumanrightsindex.org/hrsearch/displayDocumentVersions.do;jsessionid=D2B61415A51C6DCE055F77058248E836?lang=en&docId=1436 [Accessed 7 June 2009]

European Convention on the Protection of Human Rights and Fundamental Freedoms. Available from: http://www.echr.coe.int/ECHR/EN/Header/Basic+Texts/Basic+Texts/The+European+Convention+on+Human+Rights+and+its+Protocols/ [Accessed 10 June 2009]

Framework Convention for the Protection of National Minorities, Council of Europe. Available from: http://www.coe.int/t/dghl/monitoring/minorities/1_AtGlance/PDF_H(1995)010_FCNM_ExplanReport_en.pdf [Accessed 7 June 2009]

General Comment No. 23: The rights of minorities (1994) CCPR/C/21/Rev.1/Add.5 Available from: http://www.unhchr.ch/tbs/doc.nsf/(Symbol)/fb7fb12c2fb8bb21c12563ed004df111?Opendocument [Accessed 5 June 2009]

International Covenant on Civil and Political Rights (1976) Available from http://www.unhchr.ch/html/menu3/b/a_ccpr.htm [Accessed 5 June 2009]

International Labour Organisation, Convention No. 169, Article 14. Available from: http://www.unhchr.ch/html/menu3/b/62.htm [Accessed 9 June 2009]

Report Submitted by Ireland Pursuant to Article 25, Paragraph 1 of the Framework Convention for the Protection of National Minorities, ACFC/SR(2001)006. Available from: http://www.coe.int/t/dghl/monitoring/minorities/3_FCNMdocs/PDF_1st_SR_Ireland_en.pdf [Accessed 7 June 2009]

Submission by the Irish State to the Committee for the Elimination of Racial Discrimination CERD/C/460/Add.1. Available from: http://www.unhchr.ch/tbs/doc.nsf/898586b1dc7b4043c1256a450044f331/406b61b6eff7296ec1256f3900300005/$FILE/G0442321.pdf [Accessed 7 June 2009]

UNESCO Universal Declaration on Cultural Diversity, (2001) Preamble. Available from: http://www2.ohchr.org/English/law/diversity.htm [Accessed 5 June 2009]

Western Sahara, Advisory Opinion, ICJ Reports, p.12. Available from: http://www.icj-cij.org/docket/files/61/6195.pdf [Accessed 9 June 2009]

Acts of the Oireachtas

(Available from http://acts.oireachtas.ie/index.html)

The Roads Act (1993) Act of the Oireachtas, No. 14 of 1993
The Housing (Traveller Accommodation) Act (1998) Act of the Oireachtas, No.33 of 1998
The Equal Status Act (2000) Act of the Oireachtas No. 8 of 2000
The Housing (Miscellaneous Provisions) Act (2002) Act of the Oireachtas, No. 9 of 2002,
European Convention on Human Rights Act (2003) Act of the Oireachtas, No. 20 of 2003

Case Law

Mandla v. Dowell-Lee, [1983] 2 AC 548 House of Lords
Chapman v. the United Kingdom, [2001] 27328/95 ECHR
DPP v. Dunne, [1994] 2 I.R. 537
King v. Attorney General, [1981] I.R. 233

INDEX

aberrant 77, 79, 94
Aboriginal 1, 2
Aquinas 24
Australia 1, 2
Bancroft..................... ..55, 58, 60, 66
Barany 4
Bedouin 1, 46, 100
Bell 85
Bill of Rights 85
Binchy.. .... 15, 18, 19, 20
Bunreacht na hEireann 15
Canada 1, 9
Casey 21
CERD 11, 13
Cobo, Martinez 9
Commission on Itinerancy 56
Committee on the Elimination of
    Racial Discrimination
    See CERD
communitarian 54, 70, 99
Cork Examiner 72
Criminal Justice Act 1994 16
Crowley 17, 71
customary international law
    See International Law
Darfur 1, 2
Democratic 41, 43, 48, 63, 85, 98
depression 1, 34, 67, 78
dignity 15, 24-29, 43, 80
discriminatory purpose 90-92, 101
disparate impact 91, 92, 101
Dodder 16, 19, 90
Dooley v Attorney General 89
Doyle 19, 89, 90, 93, 95
Dworkin 24, 32, 33, 35
ECHR 13, 14
ECtHR 13
Equal Status Act 11, 14, 16, 89
Equality 6, 21, 51, 81, 87-101, 104

Ethnicity 12, 86
European Convention for the
    Protection of Human Rights and
    Fundamental Freedoms
    See ECHR
European Court of Human Rights
    See ECtHR
European Union 2, 4
fairs 3, 46
famine 3, 41
FCNM 13
Finland 11
Framework Convention for the
    Protection of National Minorities
    See FCNM
French Declaration of the Rights of
    Man and of the Citizen 24
Gardaí 18, 20, 21, 52, 53
ghettoisation 64
Good Friday Peace Agreement 85
Governmental Task Force on the
    Travelling Community 57
Griffin..26, 38-43, 54, 59, 61, 64, 82,
    104
Gypsies .... See Roma
Haughey 56
Holocaust 60
Honneth 34, 68, 74, 77, 83
Housing (Miscellaneous Provisions)
    Act 2002 .... 16, 90, 92, 94, 98
human person 19, 25, 28, 30, 43,
    64, 89
Human Rights Committee. 10, 12
ICCPR 10, 12
indeterminate 38, 42, 49, 59-61
Indigenous 9, 10, 13, 21, 86
indoctrination 33
Ingram 26

International Covenant on Civil and Political Rights...........See ICCPR
International Labour Organisation ..5
Irish Constitution....15, 18-21, 89, 95
Irish Times 72
Irish Travellers .... See Travellers
Israel..1
itinerants...............................3, 56, 57
Kant...24, 99
King v. Attorney General 21
Kuchis 100
Kymlicka..86
Liegeois.......................50, 54, 65, 83
Lindley 34, 36, 63, 64
Local Authorities..15, 53, 57, 76, 92, 94
Locke..8, 52
maladaptation................................65
Mandla Criteria 12
markets.............................3, 5, 46, 74
Middle East 1
Mill...37
minimum provision 41-51, 61, 75, 82
mis-recognition .... *See* recognition
Molloy.....................................19, 90
moral right.................................6, 42
Namibia..2
Native Americans..........................87
Negev Desert...................................1
Ni Shuineár 13
Niner 54
Nozick..25
On Human Rights
See Griffin
Parliamentary Debates.......19, 76, 90
pastoral..1, 3
Pavee Point....................................46
Personhood............................. 27-30
prima facie right............6, 14, 22, 24
privacy.....................................21, 48
Prohibition of Forcible Entry and Occupation Act 1971.........89
propaganda........................43, 66, 67
Rathfarnham....................16, 19, 90
Rawls...35

Report of the Task Force on the Travelling Community 17
Republican.....................................41
Roads Act..........................16, 17, 53
Roma 1, 4, 6,, 11, 49, 52, 55, 60, 69, 83, 86
Roma Gypsies .... See Roma
Roma-Gypsy.................... See Roma
Romany .... See Roma
Saami..........................9, 11, 46, 100
schizophrenia...........................34, 67
sedentarisation.51, 55, 60, 64-67, 72, 87
sedentary society.
See sedentarism
self-confidence 34-36, 68, 74-80, 83, 98, 103
self-esteem. 34-36, 68, 74, 77-80, 96, 103, 105
self-respect34-36, 68, 74-80, 98, 103, 105
social group 69-71, 94
sovereignty 9
Sunday Independent 72
Tauregs.. 1
Taylor...74
terra nullius............................... 8-10
threshold...28, 42, 48, 59, 74, 79, 82, 101
tinsmiths 2
torture 33, 63, 94, 100
transnational 4, 46
UDHR ....
See Universal Declaration of Human Rights
UNESCO..11
United Kingdom............................41
United States 41, 90
Universal Declaration of Human Rights...........................24, 25, 42
Vattel.. 8
welfare....6, 30, 41-43, 51, 55, 65, 99
Wellman...28
Western Sahara................................ 8
World War II...........................24, 85
Young, Iris Marion 69-71, 75, 86